THE
GIFT
OF
LUCK

THE 10 ESSENTIAL STAGES TO
DEEP AND LASTING CHANGE

BLAKE SUZELIS

*I dedicate this book to Jacqueline,
Seth, Caed, Jude, Eden, and Alette.*

Table of Contents

1

Setting the Stage for Success

If you are a sojourner seeking the next adventure toward personal transformation that will allow evolutionary change to ripple across the globe, then this book is for you. If you know you are destined for greatness and desire to make your mark in this world, then this book is for you. If you want to be a part of something greater than yourself, then this book is for you.

TRAVELERS BEWARE: This journey comes at a high cost to you and those around you. The price is your life! The person you now know reading this book will inevitably be changed for good. This affects everyone with whom you come into contact. Don't say I didn't warn you!

At this moment, you have a decision to make. You can stop reading because, frankly, the idea of such transformation is more in-depth than you may be prepared for or desire to go. Perhaps you are perfectly fine with how your life is going, and you fear a journey down such a path may create waves big enough to wash your castle away if you stir them up. On the other hand, perhaps you are ready for the next level of growth within you and through you. Maybe you have been waiting for a moment such as this, and the prospect of utilizing your greatest potential has sparked an excitement inside that draws you to read on.

Do you feel the energy within you growing right now? It begins deep within your chest and reaches out like light from the sun into your head, arms, and stomach. Can you feel the excitement of a different, better future than the one you have seen for yourself? Close your eyes and feel the thrill spread all over your body, charging the inside, pulling your lips upward as it seems to quench a thirst of the soul to breathe. Is your mind primed and ready to receive life-changing truth from modern science and ancient wisdom? Harness the excitement, feel the energy, clear your mind, and accept my gift to you as we adventure together.

Where do we begin? One of the challenges and most significant strengths of this journey on which you are about to embark includes building upon character qualities already within you. For example, you may want to race through this book and read it for the content, the message paper in the fortune cookie. Unfortunately, at that pace my gift to you would not be complete, nor would you build your character trait of Patience. In any previous journey worth taking in your life, Patience embodied an active part. Patience is a vital player in creating, maintaining, guiding, and walking with you through the excitement, the frustration, the successes, the failures, and, ultimately, the joy of attaining your achievement. Indeed, any journey where Patience is not welcome will lack the rich, lasting quality of greatness. It is only for your benefit that I implore you to ask Patience to join us in this journey. In the end, you will be grateful for the company, just as you have been in the past, knowingly or unknowingly, as you have built many other new skills.

Meet Patience. Let us think of Patience as a set of deep breaths. For those of you who have not met with Patience in a while, let us spend a moment getting better acquainted. If you are sitting, take a moment to feel your body against the chair and your feet against the floor. Notice any tension you have in your stomach, chest, shoulders, neck, or head. Relax and release the pressure with every exhale. Take a deep breath while counting to four. Allow the air to fill your belly. Exhale for another four to six counts and relax your body even further. If you are able and feel safe enough, close your eyes and repeat several times until you experience a deep relaxation all throughout your being.

Hello, Patience.

Witness how your body feels now. Notice the tension in your stomach, chest, neck, shoulders, and head. As we accept Patience into our company, the benefits include less stress and anxiety, better sleep, and lower blood pressure (among other gains). In this state, your mind will be more ready to receive any insight you require as if your focus doubled in capacity. Now that you are primed and ready, I have some questions for you.

Are You Lucky?

Do you think it is by luck that you are reading this book right now? Is it a coincidence? Is it a divine appointment in your journey of growth for you to make your mark in this world?

Your answers to these questions tell much about you, and we may be able to deduce (like the legendary Sherlock

Homes and Watson duo) many interesting qualities within your psyche. If you believe Luck led you to spend time in these pages, then I may surmise that in your eyes many people who are happy and doing well for themselves have been gifted moments of chance allowing them to reap life's benefits without having to work hard like the rest of the people in the world. From this perspective, Luck is a gift of chance.

In one respect, I will support your perspective such that you could allow this *Gift of Luck* to change your life, the environment around you, and the people you love. In this case, this is your chance, you only get one shot at this: do not miss your opportunity to embrace the gift that you have been given!

Two caveats, however. First, believing Luck to be a gift of chance means that only some people can obtain this life-changing gift while others continue to wait for their moment of opportunity. It is true: life is not fair. If you haven't already, accept this now, it will only help you. Some people are born into miserable or even tragic situations outside of their control, and my heart breaks for them. Is it possible for those who do not receive Luck to rise above and overcome their circumstances, creating a life consistent with their wants? Your answer to this question may be a good indication of your level of hope. If you were thinking "probably not," then it is fair to say that in many cases you view life through a relatively pessimistic lens and see little reason to work harder unless you get a gift of Luck. For those who answered positively, you have a healthy dose of hope instilled within your being, which will be of great use now and throughout the rest of your life. Safeguard your confidence, allow it to grow, and spread that hope to others. Hope is the impetus of change. Without hope, people do not move from any unpleasant dwelling spot, like a frog being slowly boiled alive in a pot.

If you tend to gravitate toward negativity and wonder if you could ever be positive and hopeful, then I can assure you that your internal voice that is answering the question in your mind right now is accurate. Our perspective on life dramatically influences the outcome. The only way to create change within you and around you is to believe that change is possible. Change is possible! The capacity to change resides in us all; in many ways, it is our perspective and fear that holds us back. It's cliché, I know, but true. It is not easy to accept the truth when you live in contradiction to that truth, because then you would have to admit to living a lie, which is not a popular or easy task. However, it is doable. Throughout this book, I will speak many hard truths, and I implore you to read them with love from the giver because I am for you! If this is one of those hard truths, take a moment with our friend Patience.

The second caveat: in believing Luck in this way, Luck is a wolf in sheep's clothing. Underlying Luck is the very belief that no matter how desperately hard you work toward a goal, ultimately the result can only be attained through chance. How disempowering! Luck robs us of our control, therefore, robbing us of hope. As we will talk more about in the next chapter, Hope and Control are forever bound together in the quest for making a difference, whereas our buddy Luck, as you now know him, steers us away from these first two key players you need to embrace on our journey.

Would you be open to believing Luck to be something

other than a gift of chance? What if I was to tell you that through our journey together, you will learn to create Luck. As opposed to waiting for an opportunity, you create it. As a result, people will call you Lucky. In truth, this is the promise of *The Gift of Luck*!

Stop for a moment and notice what this brings up within. You may feel hope and excitement brewing, as the thought that your life is more in your control than leaving it to chance. You may be resistant to this new definition of Luck because this has not been your experience. Both thoughts and feelings are welcome. Either way, you have the choice to continue reading and experiencing to see how this promise can play out in your life. You have to decide for yourself if you want to be Lucky.

Lucky Comes at a Price

The warning is real. Lucky comes at a price.

So what will it take? What expectations accompany the promise of being called Lucky? What is the cost of admission to changing your life? What is it worth to you? Let me ask you again: *what is it worth to you?* What is it worth to you to feel a change within yourself? What is it worth to you to see change within the people around you? What is it worth to you to witness your children, your grandchildren, and the generations to come in your family growing up in this place of change we are envisioning? What is it worth to you to see a difference in your community? What is it worth to you to see a transformation in our world? Sit with that for a moment. Allow these questions to penetrate past the defenses you may have put up for used car salesmen, or a friend trying to sell you on joining a multi-level marketing company. No one wants to feel as though he/she is being manipulated even if it is for a good cause. This is something you have to own for yourself. Not for me, not for your friend who gave you this book, not for anyone else. Just you. How much do you want this?

The cost is time.

The cost is commitment.

The cost is losing yourself. At least the version of yourself you know now.

The cost is figuring out how to maneuver the new version of you within your family and social circles.

The cost is making the difficult choices that feel so foreign and downright weird.

The cost is being open to something new and potentially scary. This is probably the most difficult cost to come to terms with. We grow up normalizing our situations, our family strategies, our ways of doing things, and our family beliefs. As children, we want to believe we are normal. In this journey we have to be okay with realizing that there may be different, healthier ways of doing, thinking, or merely being. I'm not going to use the word "normal" because it is a façade. Normal doesn't exist. But I promise you will never have a stronger sense of being part of a family than you will when you join this journey. You will feel: Loved. Accepted. Safe. Connected. Be a part of this family's change story.

There are many costs to a brand new life. What is it worth to you?

If you understand the benefits, if you clearly see the price, and if you still want to move forward, then commit now. I promise you will never regret a single day of it. The freedom, love, power, and connectedness you will find will be like nothing else you have ever experienced.

The question is: are you ready?

Creating Your Change Story

What do you want your change story to look like?

Believe me, we are going to make sure your change story is a story worth telling!

Before you can determine where you want to go, it is helpful to identify your current state of affairs. What is your life like now? Who are you? Which people play essential roles in your life? What consumes the time in your day? Take a moment to think about these questions and write down what surfaces. This is not a moment to worry about grammar, sentence structure, or coherence. Allow the words to flow effortlessly from your pen, as if an extension of your hand. Be honest with yourself, but do not judge. Allow grace to fill the space around you while you stare intensely inside and acutely to the life around you.

Now that you know where you are on your life's map, you can determine where you want to go. You are in good company if you do not have a clear vision of where you want to go. This step can be extremely challenging, even paralyzing for many. To help create some traction, we will begin by creating your life mission statement.

You are embarking on your own personal adventure and to know where you want to go, then you need to have an idea of who you want to be. Your mission statement will likely be unique to you, your situation, and your future. Think about these questions while you generate ideas for your personal mission statement.

What do I want to value most about life?

What do I want to prioritize in my life?

How do I want people to describe me?

What am I naturally most passionate about?

What would I regret if I did not accomplish it in my life?

If I could give a message to the world, what would it be?

What purpose is God calling me to?

Take some time with each of these compelling questions to gift yourself with a focus for your identity and purpose. This will change and evolve through our journey together, therefore do not worry about perfecting it now. Establish a basic framework to begin and allow the momentum of this change current to take you downstream as you work through this book.

Next, use your mission statement to develop your vision statement. The goal is to position your vision statement in front of you as a guiding star, beckoning you toward the unknown and drawing you into a story worth living. The vision for your future self develops throughout your life, therefore give it room to breathe without determining only a single narrow line to walk on. As you do, the scenery may look different, the people with whom you are connecting may shift, and your passions may spur you into grossly varying directions that you could never have previously imagined. I find myself more equipped mentally, emotionally, physically, relationally, and financially as my vision statement finds its way into discussions (often daily). Sit with these questions as you focus your sight on your own personal light.

What makes me feel fulfilled in life?

What would make life feel incomplete if I didn't experience it in my lifetime?

How do I imagine my ideal life? (Dream big!)

What legacy do I want to leave?

What three things do I want to pass on to this world to make it better for myself, my loved ones, and the future generations of my family?

Even writing these questions gets me stirred up and excited! Take some time right now to jot down answers to these questions. Allow this moment to draw you into rewriting the next chapter of your story. One of the hardest parts of this exercise consists of shielding against fear or constraints that can hinder the process. Perhaps: fearing what people will say, allowing age to determine your vision, worrying about finances, having to leave your home, convincing a significant other, or believing that God would never want you to pursue such a dream. Set all inhibitions, fears, and constraints aside. Open all the doors and dream big! I mean, why not? Are you afraid of being disappointed by falling short of the dream? I get that. Do you have to commit to a massive change in your life for it to feel significant? Maybe, maybe not. Only you can answer that.

Let imagination, passion, creativity, emotion, and your inner spirit take hold of your hand and sketch out in pictures or words the deepest desires of your being. Listen for a word, pay attention to your mental images, and witness what your body and soul are desperately attempting to communicate. Get to know yourself even better during this moment in time, in a more profound way, and allow Patience to be your great companion as you invest in your future self.

Hello, Patience.

(Intentionally left blank)

How are you feeling? Overwhelmed? Scared? Guilty? Excited? Allow the emotion to bubble up and breathe it out. Your ability to allow for and accept your ever-changing emotions and then to manage them will directly enhance your capacity for being Lucky.

During this journey, continue to craft an increasingly developing idea of your mission and image of your vision for this one life you have been given. The next step in the process of creating your change story is looking innovatively at your vision, which provides you with a foundation to put together your success plan. So often we keep our north-star vision in a box with all the constraints of the "probable." I'm asking you to open the box, allow the image of your future to breathe, open all the locked and unlocked doors to a different future, and bury probability while you focus on possibility. You can and will have a different future!

Think about the people who are living out their potential and possibilities. The reason they believe in change is that they are living proof. They are their own evidence. I am living proof! Who am I? I am a person no more valuable or more talented than you. One thing I have in abundance though is hope. I am willing and want to share it with every person around me, including you.

Are you willing to get rid of the box in which you live, to take a leap of faith, to trust, and to let go of any preconceived notions of how your dream could be accomplished? This is the second hardest aspect of creating your vision and plan. Sometimes we get locked in to how we think things *should* happen to take the next step in our journey. Guess how many people get stuck at this point? Countless. Are you going to be different? If you want to open that coffee shop and finances are holding you back, then it is time to think outside the box. Get rid of the box! Write down every idea, regardless of how ridiculous or impossible it seems, in your brainstorm session. Life is too short to allow any common commodity, like money, to get in the way of your vision.

Let us discuss the idea of opportunity cost. Dictionary.com defines opportunity cost as "the loss of potential gain from other alternatives when one alternative is chosen." Meaning, if you decide to spend your time watching Netflix or YouTube or scrolling through the screen on Facebook, Snapchat, or Instagram for hours, then the opportunity cost is that you could have spent your time doing something else that may have been much more fulfilling or life-giving. Therefore, you can spend time focusing on tasks or relationships that deplete your freedom and opportunity, or you can act out your mission by following your vision, creating your success plan, and taking the next step toward leaving a legacy. It is that simple, right? If only it were. However, people who are living out their possibilities spend very little time wasting the precious minutes and hours they have been given.

Broken Promises

We are going to shift gears for a moment and deal with the elephant in the room. How many times have you heard lofty promises (like the assurances given here in the few pages you have read) and been disappointed at the end when the guarantees were not realized? Probably more than you can count. Do not get me wrong, you will receive the gift of luck by our adventure's end. People will begin calling you lucky after you work through this journey, embody the practices, and witness the changes within you and around you. However, right now it is imperative to allow the fear of being deceived and the inhibition of being let down surface. Become aware of how you feel these emotions in your body. Connect with how you experience them within. Let us sit with that right now. You aren't likely lacking in experiences of the fear of being disappointed. As you connect yourself to this feeling, I imagine it to be a sincere sadness in your heart and head. It may remind you of being abandoned of hope, time and time again, after believing whole-heartedly in something, particularly when you so desperately want and need it to be true. There is more. This feeling is mixed with a tinge of guilt and anger directed at yourself and others for being vulnerable, allowing yourself to get hurt, and promising yourself that you would never let it happen again. Can you remember this feeling? Do you feel it now? Sigh. I know it all too well. It has happened to all of us. Pain's sword has penetrated into our soft flesh, wounding us all. It is the feeling of hope being trampled recklessly underfoot. We avoid this feeling of pain with every fiber of our being to stay in our turtle shell of protection. So why am I asking you to crawl out of your covering and expose yourself by sitting with this right now? Because it is real. Pain is real. The tears you feel welling up in your eyes are real. The warm stream that flows down your cheeks is real. The heaviness growing in your chest as you allow yourself to re-experience the emotion is real. And there is no shame in this. Feel it. No judgment. To feel emotion is to be human. Authentic. Real. We all crave the rawness of one another like a frantic child lost at the beach at the beginning of a storm searching desperately for their parent's protective arms, as they hear the power of the waves crashing so close and the wind pushing them to and fro. Let yourself engage with this emotion. Be human. Be raw like you may wish others would be. Take a moment right now and draw out or write out what you are experiencing. Yes, really. Feeling and processing the loss of a future that you will not have is grieving. To move forward, you need to go through the entire grieving process (denial, anger, depression, bargaining, and acceptance). Only then will you be capable of fully committing to a different future for yourself. You will thank yourself for doing it.

(Intentionally left blank)

If you are having trouble coming back down from any emotion related to this exercise, then consider one or more of the following: go for a walk, listen to some calming music, meet with Patience, talk to a friend, journal, create a collage, or one of many other choices that have worked to calm you in the past. Most importantly get it out; do not hold it in.

Allow this moment to change you. Do not steal such a gift from yourself. Until you allow this fear to exit your physical body, you cannot free yourself from it mentally, emotionally, spiritually, or relationally. Allow your meeting with pain and distress at this moment serve as a model of purging that which holds you back. Only then can you unconditionally give your whole self to your new life.

You can do hard things. No one can ever take this moment or experience away from you. Even though it was uncomfortable to go to that place, you handled it. The expression you created through your drawing showed power, not weakness. You were strong enough to do something hard, you lived through it, and now you are on the other side of it. You are better because of it. Why? So many people fear emotions, pain, and feeling uncomfortable. In this one moment, you were able to overcome that fear and allow it to impact you without disabling you. You took the emotion, the fear, the pain, and expressed it; therefore, you overcame it. You conquered it! Being proud of yourself is unquestionably appropriate. It may seem insignificant, dull, or possibly even silly, but if you think of the bigger picture of what we accomplished together, then you realize you have already begun changing your mindset toward fear, pain, and emotion.

As you experienced sadness and anger, the expression

of the emotion permitted your release and freedom to surrender to the hope bursting from beneath, which paves the path for incredible possibilities to emerge as you think bigger. Dream bolder. The change you will make in your own life is just the beginning. I'm feeling the excitement inside my body growing again. Can you feel it?

Along with your rising hope, pay close attention to the amount of control you have over your emotions. How could such a simple activity bring forth such beauty? You had some weeds in your garden, you pulled them, prepped the soil, and now you are planting new seed. You get to choose what kind of seed to plant. Do you want to plant another weed? You are so much more capable than that! Let us plant something miraculous!

A New World

As you are finding, this book is a living, breathing tool: an experience. You will discover yourself reading it over and over and finding new truths, new experiences, and new growth. Embrace it. Do not short-change yourself by skipping any moment of change. You were made for more than that. Break the cycle of stagnation and create a new path upward. We will climb the mountain together. You are not alone.

You are one prized plant among many in a garden full of weeds. As you begin your transformation, I request that you consider asking others to join you on the journey. This will create a community of change where you live. Let us pull other's overshadowing weeds to let the sun's light shine down on them just as I am going to help you accomplish this feat. In doing so, we are going to practice the exercise of paying it forward and being a part of a movement of change. Are you getting the picture? We are going to change the world! It is a lofty goal, I know. Every other book out there in this genre shares the same idealistic mission. So what makes this one any different? I'm not going to try to convince you of that right now, but if you keep reading, keep experiencing, and continue working to complete this book, you will understand how it is possible.

This is the expectation: if I can help ten people change their lives, and you are one of those ten people, then in response, you complete this experience and help ten other people transform their lives. Those ten people continue the pattern, and so on. (This is the exciting part). It only takes ten levels of change to reach ten billion people! Is your mind blown? When this truth sunk in, mine sure was. Take a second to let that settle in. Even if you help five people change, then it takes fifteen levels of change to reach the current population.

For those of you who are completely overwhelmed by the prospect of doing anything different with your life, please relax, you will still be a part of something bigger than yourself by just completing this book. Every person who legitimately and honestly experiences this journey through these pages will grow and be one more person toward the goal of changing the world. The truth is, if you find your *gift of luck* through this book, then you will want to give it to a family member, a friend, a co-worker, or one of many fellow humans struggling in the world around you. Consequently, I (and the others in this movement) will love you for it!

For those of you looking for that "something more" in life or a chance to be a part of something bigger than yourself in an even grander way, and you have a desire to create a movement that no one can stop, then I need you to do one thing: meet with Patience.

Hello, Patience.

But, don't forget your energy, your excitement, the mystery that draws you in, that raw humanness of wanting to create, the spiritual water that quenches your soul by being alongside others in a movement of change that the world has only seen through religious ministry. This is in no way intended to be a religious journey, but it could be an aspect of your faith walk. This movement is the next step in the voyage of the world as we unite! As you and the other brothers and sisters reading this book see the vision, then the result will be connectedness, just like all of the cells in a body working seamlessly together to create a deep breath. You will be aware of it and feel it. It is tangible. Just like the doubt and the fear that is inhibiting you to see the possibility of real change. Come back to the moment when you allowed the fear of deception to fall to the floor like chains. Allow that feeling of excitement to enter into your body once again, fueling the hope that is emerging inside. Feel the change. Be the change. The moment you feel hope for your future, then you have gained more control over it.

Take a week before reading the next chapter. You may need a month. Re-read this chapter a couple of times. You will only get out of this journey what you put in, and the change promised does not happen through just reading this book. You have to genuinely *experience* this book.

In the subsequent chapters of this book, I will walk you through the *The Gift of Luck* Model of Change. Each chapter will build on the next. Each section will detail the tools and experience necessary to fulfill the promise of being able to create your own Luck. The Model of Change visual concludes each chapter to help you remember some of the main points that will allow you to make the changes you are searching for.

How does Luck look now? Is Luck a gift you would like to give?

Even though I don't know your name, I love you. Although I cannot see your face, I am for you. I accept you where you are right now, and we will do great things together. Meet with Patience as often as you can this week.

Hello, Patience.

2

Foundations of Change

If you took the time to create your personal mission, you captured in writing, images, or audio the vision of where you want to go, and you can still feel the desire inside for something more than what your life offers right now, you are in the minority. And I am so proud of you! Individuals who others call Lucky savor these moments in time, these chances in front of them, as opportunities to expand, grow and make that next leap toward their new Lucky future.

If you are in the majority and you did not offer yourself the chance to gain more insight into your own mind, heart, and soul, then I implore you to stop reading right now. Go back to chapter one. Don't short-change yourself. The hard truth to accept is that you will not be Lucky unless you follow the steps involved to be Lucky. I pose the question again, are you willing to pay the price to be Lucky? I ask this for no other reason than I want what is best for you and your future! Your future self will undoubtedly thank you.

At this point, whether or not you are prepared to continue, I know you are going to read on regardless. I can't stop you. Don't get me wrong, I do want you on this journey, and you will still be better off by continuing. Therefore, let us forge ahead together!

Hope: The Fire Starter

Do you remember the attacks on the World Trade Center on September 11, 2001? If you were alive and old enough to remember what you were doing that morning, I know you can remember the feelings that accompanied that tragic event. Feelings of fear, helplessness, and hopelessness overwhelmed our nation. Even as I bring it up, my stomach begins to tighten. My second oldest son, who was not alive to experience the feelings first-hand, said that he imagined everyone felt "despair." This is evidence that 9/11 had a generational impact. That event was a moment in our nation's recent history that we can collectively say we felt unsafe. We lost faith in our nation's ability to protect us.

What do you think allowed us to rise out of the pit of fear and despair? Hope was the impetus of change in our emotions.

Hope was offered in a promise: President Bush stated, "America was targeted because we are the brightest beacon for freedom and opportunity in the world. And no one will keep that light from shining...America has stood down enemies before, and we will do so this time" Our nation took responsibility for the mistake that led to nearly 3,000 killed and over 6,000 injured that day. We learned how safety was compromised in our airports and then a vision was created for the future that was going to be different. Lastly, we acted on what we had control over by altering security measures in airports, among other tactics.

How long did it take before you trusted that you

would be kept safe in our nation? How long before you could fly without thinking about 9/11? Has the United States just been Lucky that we haven't experienced another horrendous attack similar to 9/11? It has been much more than Luck.

Here is the first takeaway: every change story begins with Hope. If you don't believe that things can be different, then you will never willingly plan for a different future. Keep our friend, Hope, close to your heart.

To be Lucky, you need to understand the difference between the two types of Hope: impersonal and dynamic. Impersonal Hope is the belief that life can be different. When you envision a different future, Impersonal Hope grows. This is a great start! Impersonal Hope is a needed fire-starter to prepare you for a blaze. This type of Impersonal Hope will likely get you through the day with a smile on your face and excitement that stretched deep down into your bones. But how will it really influence change? Impersonal Hope encourages many to view change as something created by an outside force or by chance. I don't find much hope in waiting for a chance, especially if I have no assurance that it will ever come.

A statement I often hear from Christians: I am waiting for God to open a door. If you reside in this camp, I appreciate your intention. However, what was the Great Commission? Jesus said, "Go and make disciples of all nations....and surely I am with you always" (Matthew 28:19-20). The Great Commission was not to wait; it is to go. Take courage, the text says Jesus will be with you regardless.

In either of these scenarios, you position yourself in a place of having no control. You are either waiting for someone else to change your situation, or you are waiting for a Lucky break of chance. Without knowing it, you are positioning yourself as a victim, or you are admitting to being lazy. I am not judging you for being in either place. This strategy may seemingly work for you, but since you are reading this book, I know that part of this strategy is making you miserable. If you are looking for a way out, then let us continue our journey together, and I will share what you need to do to reposition yourself.

Intuitively, you know that you need impersonal Hope. Your intuition may not realize you also need dynamic Hope. Dynamic Hope allows you to take the impersonal Hope fire-starter and set your change story in motion. Dynamic Hope is a position where you take responsibility for yourself, intentionally learn from your past, plan for a better future, and act out your plan while focusing solely on what you have control over. The main difference between impersonal Hope and dynamic Hope is Control.

Impersonal Hope opens the door to possibility and dynamic Hope equips you with the Control you need to walk through the door to make the possibility a reality.

Coming back to 9/11, how safe would you feel even now if our nation's leaders would have envisioned a safer future, but never took responsibility for what they had control over? No additional security measures would have been put into place. If they had just hoped (impersonal) that no other terrorists would try using our airlines against us and by chance we would be kept safe, then I can assure you the people of our nation would not feel secure. And, unfortunately, we would have likely suffered many more attacks as a result.

One last side note about dynamic Hope, you may have

gleaned that others do not put much faith in individuals (especially leaders) who only have impersonal Hope. People trust and will follow those with dynamic Hope during hard times and even when it is not popular!

Control

You now understand that Luck is basically worthless if you have no Control. How do you wield the power of Luck? You, my friend, learn how to create chance and opportunity.

If you boil it down, you have control over two things. First, you have control over yourself. This includes your thoughts/beliefs, emotions, actions/reactions, and your half of all relationships. Your first instinct to reading this list may be to justify how you do not always have power over these, especially your emotions. However, if you do not have control over these, then who does? Who is responsible for you?

Even though you may not always feel in control over yourself, *you* are the only one responsible for your thoughts, your emotions, your behaviors, and your half of all relationships. How often do you hear, "He made me so mad," or "I just want to make you happy?" Both statements are based on lies. No one can force you to have any emotion, just as you cannot force others to have a certain feeling, or no one can make you think about the color yellow (you just thought of yellow, didn't you?). You can *influence* and be influenced, sometimes intensely (like when people say not to think of the color yellow) but, ultimately, you choose your reaction to the situations and the people around you.

There is no victimization here. As you accept the victim

role by blaming things in your life on what other people say or don't say, what other people do or don't do, or how other people treat you or don't treat you, you are robbed of your Control, leaving yourself hopeless once again. Please recognize that as you blame others, you are giving away your power. Not only that, you are allowing others to control you! To be Lucky, it is crucial to accept Responsibility for yourself. Take Control over yourself and feel Hope surge. You will be one step closer to being Lucky!

My wife and I were married at the age of twenty-one, which was three months after our oldest son was born. We started out a little backwards, but we have learned so much since then. I used to believe that she was the only one who could make me happy because she was the only one 'to complete me.' If she did not give me a goodbye kiss, hug me long enough, or return my love just the way I thought it was supposed to be done, I felt angry and miserable. I allowed it to ruin my entire day. This quickly led to feelings of resentment and a greater unwillingness to meet her requests. I know, many issues are presented in just that one admittance. However, the point I want to make is that I was placing my wife in a terrible, impossible, and never-ending position of losing. She could not read my mind and know exactly what I wanted, exactly when I wanted it. (Notice I said "want" and not "need." Definitely an important distinction to make). Once I realized that no one else is in charge of my happiness, and I am the only one who can make me happy, I did not want to believe it. That lie held me in bondage for so long that once I accepted the truth, I knew I would have to own up to years of poor behavior. Once I did so, the freedom I received was overwhelmingly worth the repentance. Dropping those

26

chains felt so incredible!

It may seem impossible to feel such freedom. I assure you it is not. Begin by planning for success today. Tomorrow will be better.

The first move to taking Responsibility for yourself brings us to the second aspect of life you have Control over: planning for success. Planning for success spans all areas of life. If you are a student, you prepare for success by scheduling time to attend class, complete assignments, and study for exams, as well as ask for help when needed. If you are a parent, you plan for success by scheduling time to read parenting books, attend parenting classes, discuss helpful strategies with other parents you deem "good" parents, etc. If you are a spouse, you plan for a successful marriage by scheduling time to read marriage books, attend premarital counseling, participate in marriage retreats/counseling, talk to couples who have healthy marriages, assess progress, and ask for help when needed. Do you see a pattern?

You may be on the other side of the spectrum regarding feeling out of Control. Your life is overwhelming, and your schedule is bombarded with things you have to do because your completed to-dos are forever being replaced by new ones. Your calendar may seem to fill up on its own as if it is a dictator directing how your life runs. At times you may even be robbed from the joy of commitments you typically anticipate. Feelings of exhaustion lead you to desire isolation. You may feel as if you are burdened by the seemingly endless powerlessness of not living the life you really want to be living. Feeling overwhelmed just thinking about it? Ready to take back your future and regain control over the direction of your life?

To plan for success regarding taking Responsibility for yourself, begin with something my youngest daughter calls, "Check yourself." Create awareness of your body, thoughts, emotions, actions/reacions, and your half of relationships. (We will discuss this in further detail later in our journey). Then create a plan to address limiting or unhealthy aspects of you. Easy peasy! Not really. However, that does not make it any less critical. Do the best you can (not perfectly, just increasingly) and continue to focus on what you have Control over in the present moment.

How much Control do you really have, anyway? It is true that you only have Control over about ten to twenty percent of your future, but you do not want to give away even a partial percent. Hold on to it with both hands. Plan for success and watch expectantly as your future unfolds before you!

Out of Control

We discussed how you have Control over only two things, which accounts for ten to twenty percent of your future. Meaning, you have no Control over eighty to ninety percent. This a huge percentage! Conveniently, you have Control over two things, and you have no Control over two things.

You have Responsibility for and Control over yourself. Therefore, you have no Control over others, which includes their thoughts/beliefs, emotions, actions/reactions, and their half of the relationship. As a result of reading this, your feelings could be going one of two directions. You may be feeling freedom in the area of your heart and mind where guilt resides as you recognize that you are not Responsible for other adult's successes and failures. This is freeing, indeed!

However, you may be feeling your heart rate and anxiety spike because you keep yourself feelings safe and secure by attempting to control and micro-manage every person around you within reach. Unfortunately, this strategy only leads to disappointment, broken relationships, and heartache that you have fallen short of the unattainable goal you have placed before you. Imagine a dog running toward the lettuce-eating bunny in an attempt to shoo it out of the owner's garden, only to be strangled by the collar attached to the corded run. The dog just wanted to do what was right. How often do you want to do what you know to be best for someone but end up feeling used, angry, and bitter at everyone, unwilling to even offer help to others out of the fear of being manipulated again? Truthfully, you never had Control over the other person's thoughts, emotions, behaviors, or situations from the beginning, and you were attempting to rob someone else of *their* Control. Was it out of love? Absolutely! Unfortunately, this action does not result in a loving feeling inside. How do you know when you are taking on responsibilities that are not yours while enabling others? How do we know when to offer help without feeling used and resentful? Until we get to chapter four, narrow your focus to taking responsibility for your own thoughts, emotions, behaviors, and your half of relationships and the rest will be addressed at that point.

The other aspect of your future you have no Control over is the outcome. You can plan for success, do everything correctly, and the result can still be different than what you had expected.

An example I shared for years to clients in counseling was that we can plan to have a great party by crafting the menu, purchasing the food, making the food, preparing the entertainment, inviting the guests, etc. However, the night you plan the event an ice storm could make the roads unsafe and undrivable. As a result, the party would have to be cancelled. Coincidentally, a couple of years ago this scenario actually happened to my wife and I. We really have no Control over the outcome of the future!

What happens when you fixate on what you have no Control over? It only makes you feel miserable. Does it change anything about the situation? Nope. Therefore, it changes nothing, and you are killing yourself by ruminating on the eighty to ninety percent of the future you have no power over. Consequently, due to your stress level, you are less capable of handling the aspects of your life that you could be addressing and controlling. Therefore, to be Lucky (and not be miserable) you would do well to focus only on what you have Control over in the moment and discern how you can let go of that which you have no Control over.

When we find our thoughts and feelings racing out of control, this can be such a simple, yet powerful exercise that becomes more powerful the more it is utilized. Take a moment now to ground yourself in the present. Begin by reading through this paragraph, set the book down, and take one to two minutes to just be. Close your eyes and witness life at this moment as it is happening by using all of your senses. Begin with your sense of touch. Take a deep breath in through your nose and out through your mouth. Witness what the air feels like as it passes into your sinus cavity, down into your lungs, as it fills your belly and returns up and out over your tongue and past your lips. Witness how your feet feel against the ground, how your body presses against the chair, notice the softness or hardness, the texture of the chair, and the temperature in the room. Witness what the place smells like as you continue to breathe deeply. Witness what you hear. Are there any tastes in your mouth? When you are ready, open your eyes and witness your surroundings: the people, the objects in the room, the colors, and the visual textures. Do so without any judgment. Just witness your experience, as if for the first time. Lastly, witness whether or not you found yourself thinking about the past or the future for that one to two minutes. Recognize how this exercise could possibly allow you to focus on one priority at a time. Witness if and how your stress level has shifted. By practicing this exercise, you will find over time that you gain complete control over changing your stress level. You are not a victim to your circumstances. Remember, the more you take back control over your life in every moment, you also bring back hope. Allow the excitement to fill you right now. Take a deep breath and just enjoy.

Hello, Patience.

Setting Priorities

My family and I enjoy going camping, hiking, and spending time near water. Often we find ourselves spending time searching for unique rocks. Frequently, we find rocks that seem to almost call to us to bring them home, so we do exactly what the rocks ask and place them in our backpacks. As people walk into our home, they notice how we have decorated and adorned multiple surfaces with all these stones. At some point we have had to ask ourselves: can we indeed hold on to all of these rocks? Therefore, we end up tossing handfuls into the driveway with all the rest of the common rocks because we just don't have the space to keep them. As silly as it sounds, it can be challenging to choose which rocks to keep and which to toss. In those moments, we remember how extraordinary each stone had been at the time we found it, but in the end, we still have to let some go.

Imagine carrying a backpack on the walk through life, and at different points, you gather stones. You transport them on your back through the entire day at work, through dinner, while spending time with your family or friends, and even while you sleep. Some stones are given to you by people asking you to help them with their load, and as any loving and helpful person does, you take the rocks they are handing you and gently place them in your backpack with the rest of your stones. Over time you find that your backpack has acquired so much weight that you begin feeling tired as you struggle to endure the day, get through dinner, get through family time, and get to bed. Unfortunately, even your sleep isn't restful because you have the constant reminder of all of the stones in your backpack still digging into your back beneath you, leaving you tossing and turning all night. So what do you do? In the past, I would put on a smile every day as to not reveal the weight of the burden of my stone-filled backpack. I just pushed on. After all, everyone offered such positive affirmations of how strong I was for carrying such a large load. In a way, the weight all felt worth the compliments (at least for short periods).

What would it look like to sit down with your backpack, open it up, and sort through all the stones? As you begin pulling rocks out one by one, you notice how each one is a different shape, size, color, texture, roughness, and weight. Memories of the stories accompanying each stone flood your mind and stir your emotions. All of them are special in their own way, for sure. While sorting the pile, you notice something written on each stone. Your hand stretches toward a stone that catches your eye: the stone you collected as you took your spouse's hand in marriage. Letters are carved into the rock.

A name. Your name. You grab another stone and remember a friend handed it to you as you agreed to join the club for your child's school. What name is written on that? Well, that is strange, it has your friend's name. Your name is not scribed anywhere on the stone. As you fix your gaze upon the rock pile, the realization occurs to you that you don't have any more time and the rocks need to be placed back in your backpack to keep moving to the next commitment. Your heart begins beating faster, and that all-too-common feeling of anxiety extends into your chest and stomach as you think about putting all the stones back in the bag and carrying them again.

Imagine how you would feel if you began giving everyone back the stones with their names on them, and kept only the ones with your name? How much lighter would your backpack be? Would it still be too heavy? It could be time to toss some of those precious stones into the driveway with the other common rocks to be able to carry the ones that mean the most to you. The freedom of a lighter load will significantly outweigh the small amount of praise you get from transporting everyone else's stones, or even the rocks you etched your name into. Later in this book, we will discuss in greater detail how to decide which stones to toss and which to keep. For now, just begin giving back other people's stones to take the next step of planning for a prosperous future.

In addition to decreasing the weight of the backpack, using only one stone at a time throughout the day can offer a better night's sleep, less stress, and a happier, freer you. When you are with your family, take out the family stone and drop the backpack with all the other rocks by the front door. When you are at work, set the work stone out and leave the rest of them within grabbing distance. This allows you to be more engaged and mindful in the present moment. Productivity increases, anxiety plummets, self-esteem rises, guilt and resentment fall away, joy soars, and you can breath deeply and effortlessly. That is a promise!

Hope. Control. Self-responsibility. Priorities.

3

Who are you really?

Even this early in our journey together, I'm sure you can already feel more freedom as you have let go of that which you have no control over and you have reprioritized your life in a way to bring hope, excitement, and vision. Can you still feel the buzz of excitement stretching out from within you? If it has not already, it will become abundantly clear how essential both honest, nonjudgmental self-awareness and organic, unashamed excitement will change your life and the lives of those in your circles. Take a second right now and harness that energy. Feel it. Breathe it in. Let us continuously pave these positive and powerful mental, emotional, and physiological pathways for you to return to at will as another way for you to take control over your future. Don't shortchange this experience. Everything in this book is intentional to help you with your success. I want what is best for you!

I am so excited about your future and the extraordinary things you are going to do as the new version of yourself. I want to be clear, this book is written for *you*, in this time, in this chapter of your life story. At some point, you may drift off thinking about how the insight within this chapter would be perfect for someone else. When that happens, I invite you to, first, become aware that this may be a pattern in your life worth keeping in check. Second, reroute your attention back to how the information applies to you, in your story, and in this moment of your transformation. Lastly, write down the names of the people you want to share the book with and get them a copy. We "helpers" can find ourselves getting caught up in identifying what would help everyone else, but right now try not to cheapen your experience by allowing your thoughts to focus on what is intended for you, my friend. Soak it all in, continue to create the self-awareness within yourself that will jettison you into a future that you never thought was possible. You will be so grateful that you did. The future holds plenty of time for you to gift these lessons to others. Right now is your moment to be watered, fertilized, and soaked with sun and light to grow toward the best version of you.

Each page through this book will give you the opportunity to understand the mechanics of being Lucky through your own personal change experience, which will help you create a unique story to share as a springboard to touch someone else's life. Detailing your own "change narrative" will remind you of all the intricacies and successes you do not want to forget. If you have not started already, do your future self a favor and write down every goal, the details of what worked, and outline what did not work to capture your change story, which will help you learn from your past experiences. Investing in your future self reaps excellent returns on your investment. Additionally, witnessing all your areas of personal development fuels your motivation to press on toward the prize.

Owning your Identity

To be Lucky, you need to understand and be confident in who you are as a person. This is what is meant by owning your identity.

How do you define yourself? What makes you valuable? What makes you happy to be you?

Take a moment to look in the mirror right now. What do you see? A body holding a book. A body with skin and hair covered in clothing. You understand from science that underneath the surface of your skin many intricate parts are allowing you to move, function, sense, and perceive the world around you as what we all call "life."

If you haven't noticed by now, I will be upfront in saying that I do not believe in coincidence. My view of human life is no different. An interesting point I have noticed: doctors and scientists have all the organs comprising a body, inside and out, yet we cannot get them to function on our own. A scientist bringing a human form to life is what has made Mary Shelley's book *Frankenstein* so intriguing because we just cannot do it.

As you are looking at the body reflecting back, it makes sense that there has to be a spark to make your body alive. I am going to identify that spark as your spirit. The spirit acts as the energetic and electrical force supplying the physical body with the missing ingredient for functioning: the breath of life. Why is this important in your understanding of your identity? Without believing this foundational truth, it will be challenging to see the True Self and not the false version that incites a multitude of lies.

Your spirit must have come from somewhere. I am going to suggest that it was created and came as a gift from a creator, namely God. To live as the True version of yourself, you need to understand that you were created in the image of God, which is not flesh and blood, but spirit.

How could believing I am a spirit created in the image of God be the next crucial aspect of being Lucky?

To answer this question, let us dive a little deeper into three lies that surface as a result of aligning with the False Self.

Lie #1: I am my body

Once you accept that you are a spirit and not just the body staring back at you in the mirror, then your perspective can shift, enabling you to recognize a more authentic view of yourself and others. The body you see staring back at you is just a shell, a suit (of sorts) housing the real you, the spirit, or the True Self. When you do not see yourself through this lens, you define yourself by the way you look or by the way your body functions. This attempt to find self-value in these ways only ends in pain.

My story began on a dark and stormy night (figuratively and literally). I was born with a birth defect called gastroschisis where my small intestine was formed on the outside of my abdomen. At the time, few children beginning life with similar birth defects did not last longer than a couple of years due to malabsorption issues resulting with a failure to thrive. Fortunately for me, I was given the help I needed to overcome the obstacles of being born with an imperfect body. Take a second to linger on the words *imperfect body.* Allow your brain to take you wherever it needs to go right now. You may be sorting through many thoughts and emotions revolving around your own "imperfect body." You are not alone in this sentiment. Do you really know anyone born with a "perfect body?" Popular media can twist our thinking into believing there are people born with perfect bodies, but the truth remains that there is no such thing as an ideal body, regardless of what we see at the surface. We will discuss more of the biological underpinnings of motivation, but for now, it is helpful to accept the truth that every person in this world has been given an imperfect body, a flawed shell, a broken tool housing the True Self to use and attempt to manipulate.

Think of your body as a garden tool, a rake for example, that someone gave you to use to manage a garden for them. When you begin to prepare the soil for planting, you realize some of the tines of the rake are bent and others missing. When you push the rake down against the earth the handle cracks at the base where the wood meets the metal. You can use duct tape to keep it functioning, but the longer you use the tool, it becomes clear that the rake will continue to deteriorate over time and eventually will prove to be useless. Further, regardless of the gardener's expertise, the rake can be embarrassingly unreliable at creating straight lines, evening dirt, or completing the needed tasks. Actually, it can hinder you in multiple ways. However, the rake was a gift. The owner only gave you one, and you have to work with what you have.

I'm sure you understand the metaphor of how your body is like the broken rake, and the gardener is the True Self. Think about your own life and your relationship with your body. Notice how your body acts as a tool to use and to care for. Unfortunately, it does not offer exactly what you want or need all of the time.

Bring your attention back to your reflection once again. You may say that your body looks heavier than you want, has less hair than you want, sags more than you want, is weaker than you want, does not perform like you need, or one of a host of other imperfections. Even those who everyone believes to have a perfect body would think similar thoughts. Yes, really! The good news is that you are not your body. Your True Self is the spirit within the body looking back at you, attempting to wield the tool the best way possible.

Take a moment to witness what is coming up for you right now. Perhaps it makes sense to set aside this book to wrestle with this lie you have believed as truth. Before you leave this chapter, make sure that you can honestly say that you are not your body.

Lie #2: You are not your behaviors

How well can you use a broken tool? Just *good enough*. How perfect can you get a garden with a broken rake? Only *the best you can*. Can you have perfect behaviors using a broken tool? Nope.

How often have you beat yourself up for not doing something well enough or maybe not doing something correctly? Have you ever beat yourself up for making a mistake at work or school, saying the "wrong" thing to your significant other, parenting poorly, or pushing people away from you when all you want is for them to draw close? Perhaps you don't identify with any of these or other forms of extreme self-inflicted guilt and shame. The opposite could be true, as well. If your life has reflected the attitude that "I don't care" or if you have had a string of behaviors showing that you have given up, then you need to consider the possibility that you have been driven by a fear of failure. This is still believing the lie that you are defined by your behaviors.

What is good enough, anyway?

If you cannot be perfect, then what is *good enough*? Can you use statistics to justify *good enough*? For example, is 80% *good enough*? 90%? 60%? To my knowledge, no "good enough percentage standard" has been generally accepted for all behaviors. I imagine it would be generally accepted that the percentage would change from situation to situation, person to person, or moment to moment even. My percentage for truth-telling will be really high, whereas, my percentage for practicing reflection with everyone during every conversation is easily much lower. What about acceptable percentages of loving others, encouraging others, or time spent with others? Due to the subjective nature of a "good enough standard," can we agree that even picking an ambiguous percentage seems futile? If you create acceptable percentages and rules around every behavior in your life you will drive yourself and everyone around you crazy. Are you that person? Do you want to choose to continue to be that person?

What would happen if you focused less on the ways you judged yourself and concentrated more in the moment on doing your best? Your best will change from day to day. When you are physically ill, then you will be much less likely to be the person you really want to be, however, that particular day, in that moment, that *is* the best version of you.

Can you always be proud of the best version of yourself, regardless of the quantity or quality of your work? Can you do better than your best?

What would it look like if you were able to give yourself and others grace around behaviors? Since you are a created spirit trying to manipulate a broken tool, it makes sense that you could never expect perfect behaviors from anyone. Not even close! Does this give you permission to throw away all of your moral and ethical self-boundaries and do whatever you want? Well, you could, but you will still be subject to the natural consequences of this world because you are still responsible for yourself. My suggestion is to do the best you can, accept that this present act is good enough, and recognize that you are continually growing. As you incorporate these self-talk strategies, guilt and shame will have lost a stronghold on you, which will allow you to leap toward a better, Luckier version of yourself.

Lie #3: I am my past mistakes

How do you define the words failure or mistake? Failures and mistakes can act as weights that attach themselves to your ankles, immobilizing you. What if you changed your perspective on how these words influenced you? Indeed, you cannot go back and change any past thought or deed no matter how much you desire it. Memories may be coming up right now of decisions you wish you would have done differently. Me, too! Buckets upon buckets could be filled with tears of regret. Therefore, you are in good company.

If you find your mind becoming hypercritical of your

less than performance in those moments and reminding yourself of who you *should* be, then you will likely notice the increased level of anxiety and depression that quickly follows. An overly critical nature often influences an even less productive best version of you in the end.

What do you do with all of these poor past choices? Well, you have no power over changing the past, but you do have Control over learning from these experiences. So when you did or said that thing that resulted in what may have been a life-altering moment, all you can do is learn how to avoid getting yourself into that same situation again. Instead of calling it a mistake, a failure, or any other label, you have the option of calling it a *learning experience*. Does changing the name of it change the past? I wish. However, calling those moments "learning experiences" can sure change the future! As you forge a new future focused on learning experiences, you begin to recognize your lack of power over changing the past, and more importantly, you realize the potential you have in guiding your future.

Can you always do better? Regardless of the answer, all you can do is learn from the experience and plan for the best outcome in the future, even though the final result is out of your control. Therefore, take each moment as it comes, plan to be the best version of yourself and practice accepting it in the moment. Afterward, the cycle starts all over again. We are moment-to-moment people, witnessing, learning, planning, and doing our best in each moment given to us.

Sifting through the details of those life-altering moments initiates the process of gaining control over your future because you recognize the rut you have created by continuing to try the same strategy in other situations. (Dr.

Phil said it best) *How is that working for you?* This is a question I ask myself often to become aware of what I need to learn. After reframing your past experiences, you have the opportunity to plan for a more prosperous future. This changes those future strategies and allows you to break free of the chain keeping you running around in a circle. You can choose at this moment to get off the chain. You have the power! Start by looking at your past decisions, learning from any and all choices both resulting positive and negative outcomes, devising new strategies to avoid repeated adverse consequences, sticking with tactics that have caused positive results, and creating your success plan to use these strategies for a better future.

Witness how this feels in your body right now. You may be feeling the positive energy of freedom as you accept this new model of mindfulness for yourself in your life. You may witness images of the chains of guilt and shame falling to the floor as you walk away as a free person. As you head out into the light of a new day, you can feel the warmth of the sun against your skin. Peace emanates your being.

Hello, Patience.

Or, you may be sitting there thinking that I have got to be one of those weird, free-spirited, hippies for continuing to bring up self-awareness of mind, emotion, and body. You may still be reluctant because you have always guilted yourself into action. What does that feel like in your body? Heavy, dark, and sad. Of course, you never want to be in tune with your body if it feels like that all the time! Your body longs for feelings of light, love, peace, and hope, but you cannot seem to figure out why you cannot feel that way. Listen to what your body is telling you. It is whispering to you that there is another way. If you need to reread this chapter over and over until you can accept the free gift we can all have (even you!), then you are worth that extra thirty minutes, two hours, ten weeks, or even twelve months. Do not skip over this. Do not pass go, or collect two hundred dollars. Your future self, again, will thank you for the investment you make today. This point cannot be overstated: You are worth it!

Take a moment to revisit your place in front of the mirror. Look at yourself. What do you see now? Just a body. There is no failure here. Some say the eyes are the gateway to the soul. Look into your eyes. Look deeper. Search out your True Self, the essence or spirit inhabiting the body; the true you that was created in God's image; the true you that makes you so valuable. No mistake, no imperfect body, no past can taint your value even a bit! Listen to your body, it knows the truth of the authentic self that inhabits it. You are inherently valuable!

Mirroring Your Inherent Value

You were created with inherent value, not because you deserve it, or because you are more valuable than other people. Our value was and continues to be a gift! We are all equally valuable; no one person is any more or any less precious. How does that resonate within you right now? Perhaps you want to believe you are inherently valuable, but that truth seems as though it could only be true for other people. Maybe it feels untrue because for so long you have felt and believed that you are permanently damaged and could never be as good as others. Why? Because you continue to base your value and identity on the false version of yourself. You find your identity on what you do not have, what you have not achieved to this point in your life, or how you have dug such a pit that the heaviness of poor choices has confined you to a deep hole forever. Perhaps I have it all wrong, and you began life in a family that has built their lives in the pit, and the hopefulness of believing anyone in the family could have value seems unfathomable.

From another angle, you may think that believing you are equally valuable to others seems untrue for an entirely separate reason. It is not true because you think you are unique and you actually do have more value than others. Why? It's the exact same reason: you are basing your identity on the false version of yourself. You may have more education, more responsibilities, more successes, better behaved children, a more maintained yard, higher income, better job, altruistic choices, or choices that lead you to more success. Your choices in this life can lead to a much happier, healthier, and more fulfilled life than those around you, but that does not mean you are more extraordinary or valuable than others. All this means is that you have been given a gift. Enjoy the gift! But, be cognizant of when you are judging others because they have not received the same present. You made the choices, and your hands completed the task. I love hard work! Yet, you have been given the gift of a healthy mind, specific talents, the eye to see opportunity, etc. Count them all gifts. You will experience ineffable joy this way. If you see everything as a gift, then you will indeed feel Lucky!

Do you reside in either of the camps above? Do you see only the False Self and buy into the lie that you have no inherent value equal to others? Or, do you see primarily the False Self and buy into the falsity that you have more intrinsic value than others? Both are equally devastating to you and negatively impact your life and the lives of those around you. Take a moment, to be honest with yourself. Look back at the mirror. Truly look within. The authentic version of yourself, or True Self, establishes an identity in the understanding that all humans were created equal. This does not change. We may have different roles and responsibilities in this life, but we are all equal. The rest of life is based on the chance of which family you were born into, and the natural (albeit positive or negative) consequences of our moment to moment choices, which we will address more in later chapters.

The only way to see the True Self, your inherent value, and the intrinsic value in others equal to your own is by being honest. This may be a valid point to stop and journal about the thoughts and feelings surfacing. If nothing else, take a moment with Patience.

Hello, Patience.

Self-Acceptance

Why is it so crucial to comprehend inherent value, equality, and the True Self? Only then can you see yourself *and* others clearly. It is one thing to understand and accept yourself for who you are. It is another hard, painful step to accept without reservation, without judgment each and every person around you. And the only authentic way you can fully accept others is by fully accepting yourself first. The only way to accept yourself is by understanding, seeing, and believing the True Self within you. What happens afterwards is something you will find deeply meaningful. You are able to accept the True Self as your identity. To make it even sweeter, you begin seeing the true identity of everyone around you; an identity that is not based on beauty, style, poor choices, great choices, good behaviors, bad behaviors, a tainted past, a successful past, or any other aspect of the False Self. At this point, no one's identity is based on a label of good or bad. At this moment, *behavior* is the only thing to label as good or bad. You can then accept a person where they are in their journey while still approving or disapproving of their behavior, yet not falling prey to it. Finally, the fault-finding voice guilting you into doing more and more gets softer and softer, which influences you to be less critical and more likeable to others.

It is human to see the natural consequences of others, whether they lead to success or to ruin. It is human to want to gravitate towards those who are succeeding, in hopes that it will rub off. We tend to push away those who are severely struggling, due to poor choices, as to not get stuck in their stagnation. Witnessing these phenomena around us is human. But, you have the opportunity to judge them or to accept them in their journey's moment. Remember, just like you, they are no less equal in value or any different in their identity of the True Self regardless of their temporary place in time and regardless of what got them there.

At the beginning of this chapter, I told you this book is designed with you in mind, and we are spending a lot of time talking about others. This statement still has not changed. As you see others for their true identity, you transform in ways that only can be understood by those who put on these new glasses. It is a moment-to-moment choice that we all make one way or another.

Think about forgiveness for a moment. We tend to think of forgiveness as an intentional act of letting go of hurt or pain we attribute to someone else. Acceptance goes beyond forgiving a person for a single hurt and moves you to the nature of forgiveness. A kind act is to a loving character, just as forgiveness is to acceptance. Forgiveness is not meant for the heart of another, it is intended to free you of the burden within your own being, allowing you to breathe deeper, laugh longer, smile broader, and enjoy life in a more meaningful way. The heaviness of unforgiveness, bitterness, resentment, and judgment of self and others binds you to the point of drowning.

Conversely, cultivating a heart of acceptance of self and others will allow you to walk on clouds. Is acceptance for you or others? The answer is *you*, every time.

Self-Love

So where does love enter into the story? We all need a little love story in our reading and in our lives. You are in Luck. That happens right now.

The last section focused on self-acceptance, which can lead to an acceptance of others. Once you accept your true identity, you open yourself up to love. By now I'm sure you've recognized the paradigm: love must start within you and for you. In our culture, self-love often sounds and looks very different from those who do and do not truly understand it. Self-love does not mean indulging in every thought or emotional desire. It does not mean being so self-focused that you lack the awareness to see yourself within the big picture of life. Self-love does not look like blaming your limiting choices or poor behaviors on a bad day. It does not look like overspending your budget because you deserve something special to make up for your terrible experiences. This picture of self-love distorts and perverts its real intention.

For those who are feeling a bit triggered by this, just notice it, sit with it. No need to place any value or meaning on the thoughts and emotions coming up. Consider writing down or drawing about your thoughts and feelings at this moment to allow them to process in a healthy way. And as always, Patience is waiting.

Hello, Patience.

So what is self-love? It is a deep appreciation for the gift of your True Self from the creator. God is fully love. He created you in His image and you, too, have the capacity for love through the gift He has given you, which is the true you. You are the gift! He built in the capacity to be grateful enough to take care of this gift and meet the needs of this gift. In other words, you were given a gift, and you are grateful enough to take care of that gift because of your love for the one who gave it.

We could debate what constitutes "right" and "wrong" or "good" and "bad" behavior in regards to self-love, but ultimately, it is not a behavior. Self-love is accepting the gift of you, being appreciative for you, and wanting what is best for you. Not always giving you what you want, but working to consistently deliver what you need. Most likely, gaining that wisdom and turning that wisdom into practice will be a moment-to-moment journey lasting your lifetime.

Therefore, self-love precedes other-love, self-acceptance precedes other-acceptance, and all of these are only possible as a result of accepting the True Self as your true identity and as others' true identities, which never changes based on behaviors. You can, you do, and you will get angry with yourself and others, but as you recognize that behaviors lack the power to dictate whether you or another are lovable or acceptable, you will return to peace much more quickly after momentary anger. How are you currently experiencing self-acceptance, other-acceptance, self-love, other-love, True Self acceptance, or true identity acceptance?

The freedom you feel can only be perceived as you embody your true identity. It is like you have been sitting in a jail cell staring at the unlocked, open door trying to figure out how to get up and walk through. A free man, living as a slave. But the moment the truth is presented, and you decided to believe it, you stand up and walk out of the jail cell. You are not a free slave, but a free man, living free! It is already true. You are loved and accepted, which makes you loveable and acceptable regardless of the chains from the past. This is a new moment, and the future is not fixed. Embrace the True Self where acceptance and love abound while leaving behind the False Self based on lies. The True Self frees you from focusing on who you are not and allows you to focus on who you want to be!

A new life awaits.

Are you ready for it?

True Self Identity. Self-Love and Self-Acceptance.
Hope. Control. Self-responsibility. Priorities.

4

What drives you?

What would the world be like if the True Self was everyone's identity? What a difference it would make, focusing on doing the best you can versus criticizing yourself and others for who they are, who they are not, what they do, or what they do not do. Recognizing that almost all people do not intentionally try to make mistakes, be mean, parent poorly, or act foolishly. Empathy would abound. Picture a family that loved and accepted each other regardless of personal imperfections, a community that worked together for the greater good, and a nation willing to learn from its past and planning for a more fruitful future for everyone. It seems idealistic as we look at the current state of our world. Yet, isn't it a place you would want to live?

What would be the first step in working toward such an awe-inspiring change?

In one word: You.

Theoretically, it makes sense that each of us must take responsibility for ourselves, changing our own thoughts, emotions, behaviors and relationship strategies, to create a movement of change that could reach the globe. This movement begins by looking at your own hope, control, responsibility, self-acceptance, self-love, other-acceptance, and other-love. When you acheive this point of growth, amazing things can happen! However, such growth does not always happen, does it? Why not?

I remember when I asked this question to myself in my own life. Up to that point in my life, I had worked unceasingly to experience tremendous growth in these areas above. As a result, I felt good, and my private counseling practice was going well, but something was still missing. Something was still holding me back from being Lucky.

Living Fearlessly

One of the most significant struggles humans have is the fight against Fear. No greater foe exists. Fear resides at the root of countless problems, gnawing away at the immense strength we as humans have (yet all too often the capitalization of such potential fails to be converted into action). Overcoming Fear may be equally one of life's supreme challenges and most glorious rewards. Indeed, it is always a lifelong battle. In truth, reaching your highest potential only becomes a reality when you become committed to overcoming Fear.

Growing up, I protected myself by being afraid of many things in life, including being afraid of people, animals, the city, swimming in murky water...the list goes on and on. This strategy worked for me in many ways until I reached my thirties, though I did not recognize the countless ways these (and other fear-based strategies) held me back. Even though the Fears were protecting me and acting as a strength, they were the basis of my greatest weaknesses as well. I missed out on many experiences due to my Fear. I stayed safe, but at what cost? I was staying safe at the cost of being able to reach my full potential as a person, a spirit, a husband, a father, a friend, and a therapist. It has been said, "Fear leads us to trade life for existence." My goal had been (and remains) to be in pursuit of the best version of myself. How could I become the best version of myself if I was not willing to face my Fears?

Throughout my journey of becoming a therapist, I was forced to confront and overcome one of the greatest Fears humans face: the Fear of people. We try to keep ourselves safe from being hurt by others by constructing protective walls using Fear as the building material. My building blocks included: the Fear that people would not like me, the Fear that I would be rejected or abandoned destined live a lonely life, the Fear of being ridiculed, the Fear that I could not "do life" without certain people, the Fear that I would not find that special someone, the Fear that I would screw up my kids... The list drudges on and on for miles of how multitudes of Fears revolved around the *people* in the world.

The first and hardest Fear of people I needed to address was the Fear of not pleasing others, making them upset, and then, ultimately, being rejected. Have you had a similar experience? The best version of you ceases to exist when you are drowning by the need to be perfect or "good enough." Most people do not recognize the extent to which these two Fears debilitate people all around the globe. Even though these Fears may have dictated your thoughts, emotions, behaviors, and relationships for years, I can assure you that the possibility of overcoming them is real. At this point, just recognize what is coming up within you, write it down (without giving any meaning, value, or weight to it), and sit with the uncomfortable feelings for a moment. What is the point of this? Only when we allow ourselves to feel will we be motivated to change. It may be helpful to stop, take out a journal, and intentionally write out everything that you are thinking and feeling in this moment. Add an entry into your Change Story. Your future self will thank you for your investment.

Hello, Patience.

Strategy #1: Speaking truth

How do you begin eliminating the Fears of not being good enough, the need to be perfect, or other self-limiting, Fear-based beliefs? Placing personal growth as a priority in your life and working toward recognizing areas in need of growth are steps one and two. When you are dealing with these Fears, you have a tendency to avoid growth areas within yourself because growth feeds right back into your Fears of not being perfect or good enough. You get caught in this cycle of being afraid of failure and then avoiding areas of growth because they feel like a failure. In response, you build walls in your life to protect yourself from those feelings of failure, which continue feeding the very Fear that would set you free if you challenged it. You are not alone. I know it well because I have lived through it. Meaning, you have a Fear-conquering leader to guide you! Open yourself up to hope because we will get through this together.

As previously stated, Fear has a protective factor to keep you *feeling* safe, but unfortunately, the feeling represents a false sense of safety. The benefits from this false sense of security come at a high cost. However, this can be your moment. The hour you decide that you have lived your life under the oppression of Fear too long. You have the opportunity to take the reins from Fear with both hands. Let us shine a light on Fear to defeat the bodiless shadow. Reset your compass. Arm yourself with the sword of truth and prepare to overcome the evil tyrant wreaking havoc on your life. Are you ready to be free of the Fear that drowns your potential? Are you prepared to take another step toward the best version of yourself?

I have come to find that so much of Fear is rooted in lies with the guise of keeping us safe. Of course, you want to stay safe. I want you to be safe. Yet, believing you have control over your safety is not entirely accurate. You have control over planning for a safe future, but the reality stands that you have no power over the outcomes in life. This is a harsh truth, yet crucial to accept. What will it take for you to be okay not having control over the future's uncertain outcome? You will discover the truth by the end of this chapter, but you need to fully understand your nemesis.

Fear is a candy-coated lie. Let us look at the Fear of people as an example. The Fear of not being liked or not being accepted by everyone is expressed in your behaviors as striving to be perfect. You think that if you can just do _____ (fill in the blank) flawlessly, then you will be accepted. Your drive to be perfect is futile. Perfection is unattainable! Just like perfection, being liked or accepted by everyone is impossible. You will forever be spinning your tires to move out of a place of not being liked or accepted by everyone, and no matter how hard you press down on the gas pedal, you will not budge.

The Fear of not being *accepted* by everyone can only be overcome by believing the truth that you are *acceptable*. Being acceptable is all you have control over anyway. Remember our discussion of hope, control and taking responsibility? You are capable of believing that you are acceptable without having someone else accept you. You can take responsibility for what you have control over (which is your beliefs) and change them to believe that you are acceptable. Because you are acceptable! How do you alter this belief? One way includes speaking truth against the lie. The lie states that you need someone else to approve of you to be acceptable. Do you recognize how Fear can blur your entire perspective?

A friend and therapist mentor told me that twenty to thirty percent of all people will not like you no matter how hard you try to get them to like you. As a result, if you stood in a room of ten random people, then two or three of them will not like you. And that is okay. Why? It is human nature. If you were completely honest with yourself, you would recognize that you would not like or really want a relationship with two or three of the people in the group of ten either. This is not wrong or bad, it is just the way humans are in this world. The truth stands that you are already acceptable regardless if twenty to thirty percent of the population communicates a lack of acceptance of you.

Further, you can love and accept others with whom you do not connect, without needing to spend large chunks of time with them. If you feel the need to gain those two to three people's approval, you end up wasting all your time trying to prove your worth to them to get them to like you. This often leads to coming across as trying overly hard and can often be perceived as being annoying. In the end, they will still not like you. But, that is okay. You will find more joy in spending time with the seven to eight people who do desire your company, as opposed to wasting time on people who couldn't care less. It is your choice!

The hardest part of really believing you are acceptable when looking at your past or present relationships is that you may recognize that there are likely family members that fall into the twenty to thirty percent of people. It does happen. Many people believe that family should be perfectly accepting, but the unfortunate reality suggests otherwise.

You may also experience that the percentages are flip-flopped, and only twenty to thirty percent of people care to connect with you and seventy to eighty percent want to have nothing to do with you. At that point, you need to look at your communication styles, which we will discuss in chapter six. This does not make you unacceptable, it just points to the need to learn different strategies of relating. We will increase that percentage, just do not give up.

Using the strategy of speaking the truth against the lie will change your perspective over time as your life experiences catch up and confirm your new belief. When you believe the truth that you are already acceptable, a fascinating yet beneficial side-effect occurs: you begin trusting yourself. As a result, you start to believe and trust that not only are you *acceptable*, but you are *capable,* as well. Before the shift, you may have met aspects of your life with confidence when you could accomplish specific tasks well, for example, performing at work. However, trusting yourself with the totality of your life feels strikingly different. Self-trust and believing you are capable of being successful at your life, as the responsible person in control over your thoughts, emotions, and actions, throws a harrowing blow at the face of Fear. Imagine looking at your body in the mirror, into the eyes of the true you, and seeing someone who is strong, trustworthy, and capable, not just because you are good at your job, but for the fact that you are capable of taking responsibility for what you have control over in your life. Feel the weight of the chains of Fear slip off your body and fall to the floor as you become even lighter.

I desire for you to reach your highest potential and be the best version of yourself that is possible in this lifetime. Until you have tasted the sweetness of a peach, you do not know what you are missing. Only when you have experienced life with increasingly less Fear can you understand the freedom that accompanies it. Someone can tell you all about it, but when you take their hand and join them, only then, will you really get it. And it is so good!

Strategy #2: Trust

When I recognized the dire need to address the onslaught of Fear in my life, I made a firm commitment to myself not to allow Fear to dictate my decisions any longer. At that time, I was a couple of years into my private counseling practice while managing the family health food store and helping run the family alternative medical clinic and gluten-free café. Further, my wife and I had taken on co-leading a marriage class at church, taught monthly sushi classes, hosted small groups in our home while attempting to upkeep a large house, six acres, fruit trees, berry bushes, grape vines, multiple raised garden beds, and rabbits. Phew. My heart is racing just thinking about carrying all the stones I stuffed in my overloaded backpack! My wife and I had been talking about the need for change because our minds, bodies, spirits, and relationships could not handle such a stressful way of living. When we decided to move our family of seven from Ohio, where we were born, raised, and lived our whole lives, to Wenatchee, Washington (twenty-three hundred miles away) the natural consequences of such a choice rippled through the family and the community. Few supported us in our decision, and I did not blame them for that. Some thought we were running away from responsibility and into the arms of Fear, whereas my wife and I saw leaving as an act of overcoming Fear. Leaving everything and everyone behind by taking a leap of faith into the unknown is hard and scary. I never said overcoming Fear would be easy or make people happy. The results, however, are unfathomable.

Just as self-acceptance and self-love open the doorway to other-acceptance and other-love, you will find self-trust opens the door to other-trust. However, the key to the door of other-trust is the belief that the True Selves of all people are inherently good. In reality, the True Selves of all people are not malevolent or malicious. Some people believe they have no choice but to get bigger or scarier than everyone around them to feel safe (which we will talk about more in the following chapter), yet at their core and the True Self level, they are inherently good. As previously discussed, the True Self was made in the image of God, so of course it is good. Therefore, the next step to obliterating Fear's grasp on your life consists of trusting others for what you have no control over. Which past relationships and experiences are holding you back from trusting others?

To make such a tactical maneuver against Fear, you must understand the inverse relationship between Fear and

Faith, which stems from your embrace of Trust. Remember, the feeling of safety is a mirage. It is a false sense of security because you have no control over the outcome of the future. You *do* have control over trusting that God is working out His good purpose in you as you love, seek out, and accept guidance from the One who has ultimate control over future outcomes. Therefore, you can choose to place what you have no power over anyway into the hands of God, who does have control over the outcome of the future and who wants what is best for you. You thereby gain more control over your life by way of substitution. If God is for us, who could be against us?

Further, other-trust recognizes that other people are lovable, acceptable, and capable of taking responsibility for what they have control over. It also includes trusting that God wants what is best for you and has control over the future outcome. When you add both of these together, they make up all that you have no control over. In summary, to decrease Fear, you must increase Faith by way of other-trust.

My wife and I had faith that we were meant to show those around us the results of living a Fearless life. My grandmother boldly prayed that if God's will were to take us away from our family in Ohio to a place without family, then the sign would be that our home would sell the first day to the first person who inquired. Days later on Facebook, I posted my house for sale without a realtor. Within fifteen minutes, I received a reply, which eventually turned into a purchase. This is one of the countless blessings we received while trusting through Faith and letting go of Fear.

If you are really struggling right now with the idea of trusting through Faith, I am not ignoring that this is a tremendous roadblock to accepting and believing the model of change that I am sharing. This is really hard for you! I get that. You may be having strong reactions of anger, sadness, feelings of being let down, perhaps even a longing for what it feels like to have Faith or a multitude of other thoughts and emotions. Still no judgment. I have only love and acceptance. I cannot take these thoughts and feelings away, but I can be here with you as you experience them, explore them, sit with them, and attempt not to judge yourself or others as you grow through it. You may need more time for the topic of Fear and Faith to marinate, therefore, take the time you need before moving onto the next section. This moment is always a perfect time to meet with Patience.

Hello, Patience.

Fearlessly Pursuing Your Purpose

Why am I here?

What am I supposed to do with the time that I spend on this Earth?

Mark Twain stated, "The two most important days in your life are the day you were born and the day you find out why." Each of us attempts to find meaning in this life through something. For example, many find meaning in their life's work, travel, their marriage, their kids, their home, their faith, etc. No matter what, you strive to answer the questions above as you live moment-to-moment through your life to make sense of it. Some research has shown that believing you have a calling and acting out that calling directly correlates to one's view of the significance of one's life. Social connectedness, feeling happy, and, thirdly, having a way to make sense of life have also been studied and shown to help you feel as though life has significance. Ghandi stated, "The best way to find yourself is to lose yourself in the service of others." As a culmination of the research I've studied, the wisdom I've read, and my life experience, I have concluded that living out meaning in life looks like *working with others as a part of something bigger than yourself which connects you with people and the divine.*

Both Fear and Faith play critical roles in answering personal questions of significance and purpose. We know Fear hinders you, while Faith propels you. Fear limits your possibilities, holds you captive, and confines you to a little box that feels safe yet imprisons you, a free person, to live as a slave to Fear in a false sense of security. Your foundation of Faith governs your view and the way you act out your purpose.

As I shared earlier, I was born with a birth defect. What I did not share was that the doctors only gave me two to three years to live. At that moment in history, gastroschisis usually led to malabsorption, which in turn created a failure to thrive. My mom did not accept such a hopeless outcome for my life. She prayed and was directed to an alternative medical clinic where I saw a practitioner who primarily utilized homeopathy. His name was Dr. King, the owner of King Bio homeopathics. Within days of the first visit, my color changed, and I began to gain weight. At that time, I was one of the few who survived, and I always had a feeling that I was saved for a purpose. The next hardest step has been identifying that purpose.

Growing up I believed that God had one perfect path that each of us was to strive to walk, which felt like a tight-rope. If you stepped just a little one way or the other, you were out of God's will. As you can imagine, Fear abounded in my life because if I made the wrong choice as to what I thought God was guiding me to do then, I was not going to live out his will nor find true meaning in my life. What a lot of pressure! You may be feeling that right now.

The moment I chose to live Fearlessly, I knew that this view of God's will and his purpose for my life was illogical. How could I live in so much Fear (which hinders us) and still reach my maximum potential? Something did not add up. What seems like the next day, I was driving home from work and, as I often did, I put on a sermon from Alistair Begg (who has a church in Chagrin Falls, Ohio). The title of his message on that particular day was "Celebrate Life." Much wisdom was found in that message, but the overriding nugget I took away was to "Go for it!" A simple paraphrase could be that young men should pursue their dreams while keeping their eyes fixed on God. I downloaded that message, which is still on my phone to this day. Over and over I have listened to the sermon and shared it with others. My beliefs about the tight-rope began to change. I realized that I was actually walking on more of a road. I found so much hope and excitement in that! I understood the gifts and desires that God instilled within me, but until then I did not feel like I had the permission to follow my ambitions because of the Fear that suffocated me. Since then, I have been able to breathe deeper, live freer, and trust God to direct me as I follow the passion instilled within me, which allows me to reach my fullest potential. What chains of Fear are loose enough to drop right now? Let them go.

What seems very real to me is that God has prepared

me through my journey to step away from Fear and into Faith to gain the knowledge of current research in science, the ancient wisdom of scripture, mixed with my personal experience and those with whom I've counseled. All of this together allows me to be able to offer *The Gift of Luck* as a way to bring about change within me, my family, my community, my state, my country, and, ultimately, the world. You are one of the Lucky recipients!

Risky Business

How comfortable are you in your current place in life? Comfortability by its very nature often opposes change. As you are striving to be Lucky, recognize that you experience growth as a byproduct of change. Therefore, assessing for comfortability can be a springboard for determining where in your life you need to shake things up. You may not even know how the newness will influence your personal growth, but I promise, you will gain an education whether you like it or not.

What aspect of your life is a little too comfortable?

Lucky people take risks. Payoffs are directly proportionate to risk. Meaning, tremendous gain typically can only be achieved through tremendous risk. Lucky folks are willing to lay it all on the line for the sake of their purpose. As a rule of thumb, those who are Lucky are not only in it for the gain, they enjoy the game. The game is where meaning and significance is actualized.

The ability to risk significantly as a way to further your purpose takes the two main components discussed throughout this chapter: Fearlessness and Trust. If you are not able or willing to overcome Fear, in addition to Trusting yourself, others, and God, then the opportunity for possibility will be replaced by excuses for inactivity. If you are serious about being Lucky, chances you create will need to be acted on decisively even when uncertainty is present. As a result of your planning and investment, opportunities will likely not take you by complete surprise, but you need to be prepared to act the moment they surface.

You know me well enough to understand that I do not endorse jumping blindly into the unknown (even though life sometimes requires such Faith). Calculate risk according to the expected payoff and purpose you have envisioned. Such planning will tolerate high risk and high payoff.

When I moved across the country, I preceded my family by six weeks to secure a place to live. The housing market at the time was absolutely ridiculous! To explain, I bid asking price on multiple homes the same day they became actively listed, only to be outbid by tens of thousands of dollars each time. After five full weeks, I still had no place for my family to land. It was a Saturday morning, and they commenced the week-long trek to Washington. My conversation with my wife revolved around being Fearless and Trusting that God would provide. That afternoon a rental surfaced, and I happened to be the first respondent. The homeowner indicated that the house would only be available for a month because it was in the process of being sold. I accepted the terms out of sheer desperation. Two weeks later, the owner contacted me because the sale of the house fell through. We bid against multiple other people, but because we were already in the house, the owner agreed to sell it to us.

The choice to bring my family of seven across the country while leaving everyone and everything I ever knew was risky. I choose to be Fearless even in moments that seemed dire. I had to Trust myself that I had what it took to be successful. I believed that my wife was capable of handling the stress of the journey. We had Faith that God would work out everything for our good and His glory.

Life would have been so different if we had not taken the leap of Faith. In truth, *The Gift of Luck* would never have been written. Neither you nor I would have learned the art of being Lucky.

What are you feeling within you right now? What is your body telling you? How is your spirit guiding you at this moment? As we discuss Fear, Faith, significance, and risk, are you feeling hopeful? Frustrated? Excited? Sad? Confused? Overwhelmed? You are likely feeling many emotions all at once. This is human. No need to judge the feelings as good or bad, just witness. Take a moment to write down what is coming up for you at this moment. Don't skip these treasured times to stop, emote, reflect, and grow. Your time is now.

Hello, Patience.

What will your leap look like?

Perhaps you are feeling a shift within you where you sense that something needs to change in your life. Somewhere deep within, energy is growing as you understand the need to live out this one life without Fear controlling your every footfall. Are you ready to stand up and walk out of the cell that has held you captive for far too long? Embrace the inner need to live out a life of purpose. Let go of the constraining thoughts that you cannot do something different. Defeat the lies with truth. Allow Faith to grow and Fear to die. Prepare for calculated risk and overwhelming gain. Place your purpose in front of you and run unceasingly toward it. All that you have you need and all that you need you have, to make that next step happen. You can decide who you want to be right now and benefit from making every moment-to-moment choice to draw you closer to that person.

Maybe you desire to be part of something bigger than yourself. If by chance you think someone else needs to hear this message and you want to be an element of change, then perhaps it is time to share it. Partner with *The Gift of Luck* team, connect with others who believe change is possible, and change is needed. Give those you are thinking about the chance to be Lucky. Let us all change the world together! This movement will only grow. We are moving toward the end of chapter four, and we have so much more to experience together, but if you are feeling the tug inside of you now, start today. Tell someone about the book, buy someone the book, host a workshop in your area, donate to support the movement, or become a Fearless leader on our team by going through *The Gift of Luck* training program with the intention of becoming a satellite who can offer *The Gift of Luck* workshop.

Take a moment right now and write down everything you are thinking and feeling as you connect with your True Self, gain clarity around your passions, your gifts, your desires, your mission, and your vision. Witness the sense inside that you are being called to a new life of Fearless living, the desire to live out a life of meaning in a way that connects you with others in something bigger than yourself, and a future of increasing Faith. Describe in vivid detail through words, pictures, or music what you are experiencing at this moment. Allow your creativity to come through. It feels good, and you want to remember this moment as you set down this book and go about your day.

In the next chapter, we are going to immerse ourselves in connection. You are not meant to be alone. Tell someone else what you are experiencing. Let others into your world of excitement, your Change Story. Above all, make the choice today to not allow Fear to dictate your decisions any more. Be bold. You will never regret it. You've got this!

Fearless Purpose. Truth, Trusting, Faith, and Risk.
True Self Identity. Self-Love and Self-Acceptance.
Hope. Control. Self-responsibility. Priorities.

5

Connected

Close your eyes for a moment and allow your brain to think back to those who have been the most influential people in your life. Which faces appear? Who have been the wise guides in your life? Make a list of everyone who comes up. You may be thinking of a parent, grandparent, another type of guardian, sibling, best friend, spouse, teacher, coach, pastor, counselor, author, colleague, or a host of other people. What about them made a significant impact on you? Information, guidance, encouragement, safety, love, consistency, honesty, acceptance? For some of you, this exercise may be difficult because the most impactful people from your past hurt you the most and negatively impacted you at no fault of your own. Regardless of a positive or negative influence, you can learn from all of them.

How do *you* want to impact those around you? When people think of you what will they remember? This is not an exercise of condemnation, shame, and guilt, but an exercise of sitting with the feelings we have, accepting and taking responsibility for who we have been, allowing the emotions to move us to learn from our past, and planning for a better version of ourselves today and moving forward.

Lucky people are very aware of their circles of influence and intentional with the time they spend with others. This chapter will create an opportunity for you to assess your connections.

Transparency

You do not live in a vacuum. You affect those in your world, and the people surrounding you influence you, as well. In some ways, you need to safeguard yourself from the influences of those around you. Living without Fear still includes living smartly and intentionally. One way to do this is by choosing to be close to those who impact you positively while avoiding those who drag you down, hold you back, or keep you from reaching your highest potential. Who are the people in your world right now?

Another way to conceptualize the groups of people in your world is by placing them in five different levels of transparency. *Level one* includes little to no transparency: you would only share things about yourself that are meaningless, like talking about the weather. *Level two* transparency includes sharing things you know, which shows a small degree of transparency because it exposes your curiosities, interests, and how you spend your time. As you reach *level three* transparency, you begin to share opinions, likes, and dislikes, which allows you to be even more transparent because this communicates your belief system. As you reach *level four*, you become even less protected because you share your emotions, feelings, desires, passions, and dreams.

As you have gone into the deeper levels, you are

obviously more transparent, but what else increases as transparency increases? Trust *must* expand. If trust is lacking in a relationship, then it would not make sense to delve any deeper into the next level of transparency. As a result, risk also increases. The more authentic you are at each deeper level, the riskier the relationship becomes. Therefore, *level five* transparency has an inverse relationship with the number of people you allow in that deepest level. As you reach the final level of transparency, nothing is held back in the connection with the other person, and the environment consists of complete openness. These are the people with whom you could be physically, mentally, emotionally, and spiritually transparent. Due to the level of risk and to stay safe, consider choosing only one to three people at this level. Level four may safely have four to fifteen people. As you increase levels toward level one transparency, the number of people also increases.

A few points of clarification: being *authentic*, your True Self, in the moment with each person with whom you spend time is different from being completely *transparent* with them. You can be authentic with someone as you share knowledge without exposing everything about yourself. Second, the number of people you have in each level of transparency is flexible, especially in levels four and five; however, risk must be appropriately weighed. In truth, you become the most hurt from those in level five, less hurt in four, and so forth. It is difficult to remember and even harder to accept that humans are imperfect people who have imperfect behaviors. We hurt, disappoint, and sometimes damage those closest to us. This phenomenon rings even more true for those in our deepest levels, due to our degree of openness. If you are finding yourself frequently hurt, then perhaps you are allowing too many people into your levels four and five. Another critical factor to consider is not just the quantity, but the quality of relationships in your more transparent relationships.

When you were thinking about the most influential people in your world, it is possible that one or more of those individuals remain in your deeper levels of transparency now. If you have not already, write down the names of those in your levels four and five. How does each one of them influence you? What do you gain and lose in each relationship? Just witness and be honest with yourself. Observe the good and bad. Indeed, each connection has both due to our imperfect nature. Perhaps your best friend excels at praising you but falls short when it comes to reciprocity of giving gifts of time. Or maybe you encourage each other to be better spouses or parents throughout the week, yet every Saturday night the encouragement shifts to drinking substantial amounts of alcohol. It could be that you have just been friends your whole life, but most interactions with them lead you to feel frustrated and annoyed. Do your best not to judge them or make excuses for your friends, but just recognize with clarity the reality of the relationship. At this moment you may be having some strong reactions of anger, sadness, guilt, gratitude, or more likely a mixture of all of them. Take a moment to sit with the emotion. Notice where you feel it in your body. Witness their severity. Spend a moment with Patience.

Hello, Patience.

What do you do with the paper before you? What do you do with the people around you who are more of a negative than positive influence? You have the names of the most influential people in your life along with the degree of dysfunctionality and functionality. What I am NOT suggesting is that you abandon every relationship to create a stronger wall of safety around yourself. You do have a few things to consider, though. For the connections that you notice are functional and reciprocal in your life, take a moment in gratitude for them. They are special gifts that deserve to be noticed often. Possibly even send them a text, card, letter, or call them on the phone expressing your gratitude for them. I will wait.

For the relationships that you are noticing are more dysfunctional than functional, you have a few choices. First, recognize that you are half of the relationship. Relationships are dysfunctional due to both people, not just one. You have control over your half, but only your half. Take responsibility for your half.

Second, assess if you have been stealing their power or you have been giving yours away. As a refresher from chapter one, we only have control over *ourselves* including our thoughts, emotions, and behaviors. Are you expecting them to *make* you happy or do you often find yourself saying that they *make* you sad or angry? If that is the case, you are likely giving your control away through blaming. Remember, blaming is a dead-end road; it gets us nowhere.

Conversely, do you find yourself trying to *make* the other person happy? In this case, you are probably trying to steal the other person's control through pleasing. As you are only in control over your emotions, not others', all you can do is attempt to be the authentic, best version of yourself who learns from the past and plans for a better version of yourself. There is no expectation of being perfect, but work toward constantly learning and growing.

Third, if you are giving your control away, then set boundaries with yourself to begin taking responsibility for what you have control over. If you are attempting to steal others' control, then set boundaries with the other person to help them understand their power of control. What are boundaries? Boundaries are like verbal white picket fences you place between yourself and others to understand where your control ends, and the other person's control begins.

Fourth, if you get to this point and boundaries did not work, then you probably need professional help. A therapist can help you determine if a relationship is worth nurturing back to health or if that is even possible. They may help you to see that the relationship is toxic to you and it must be pruned from your life. This is where we place a brick wall and not a white picket fence. As we continue to discuss connection, you will understand the importance of pruning.

A final thought on levels of transparency can be summed up in one word: reciprocity. What if you reside in someone else's level four or five, but they remain in your level one, two, or three? If the relationship was created with the intention of one person going much deeper than the other, as in a therapeutic, coaching, mentoring, or even a parent-child relationship, then disregard the next sentence. The ideal version is to be within one level of transparency of each other. If I am a level five for someone else, then to be reciprocal, they would be in my level four or five. For example, if I have a friend who always confides in me, pours his heart out, and makes every conversation about him and does not leave room for me to share or I just choose not to share much, then there is an imbalance of reciprocity. A lack of reciprocity creates awkwardness, frustration, and feelings of not wanting to spend time with this person. No need to feel guilty about feeling this way, it is normal. But, what can be done? Ideally, have a conversation about how you do not feel heard or set a boundary of time with them, i.e., "I only have five minutes to talk."

What if you recognize that you are the one oversharing? What if you are the one who talks noticeably more than your friends? Start with sharing less. Also, create space for them to share by asking questions about them. Be authentically curious about them. Wonder what their experience of life is like in their shoes. If they still decide not to open up, then you have the option of having a conversation about the imbalance, but be prepared to listen to the frustrations of the other person, which must be heard without judgement. Do your best to repair the relationship through an apology and doing your best to make the steps towards change. Ultimately, to have a good friend, you need to be a good friend that gives and receives equally. We will discuss more regarding communication in the next chapter if you are looking for more options.

Is there more to relationships than understanding levels of transparency, control, and boundaries? Absolutely! Much more is coming. As part of that, the rest of this chapter is going to focus on understanding strategies in relationships.

Relational Strategies

As part of a holistic approach to healing and helping, often the mind-body-spirit connection is referenced. The significance of connection cannot be understated. From this moment on, I want you to consider adding another dash: mind-body-spirit-connection. Throughout the rest of this book, we will delve deeper into understanding the importance of connection and how it is equal to the other aspects of mind-body-spirit.

To begin, it helps to accept that you and I were created as relational beings. To be Lucky and become the best version of yourself, an understanding of connection is imperative, especially since current research on attachment theory concludes that children learn their relationship strategies by the age of three-years old or younger. What do I mean by strategies? Relational strategies are the ways by which we attempt to get our needs met in relationships. For better or worse, our strategies all begin with our primary caregivers.

At the not-so-ripe age of twenty, I became a father (ready or not). I had no idea what I was doing even though at that point I'm sure I would have told you (and perhaps believed it myself) that my way of parenting could be taught in the universities because of the wisdom one would gain. This was a very different version of me, so many years ago. As I look back knowing what I now understand, I cringe at so many of my parenting choices, but just like everyone else in this world, I was doing the best I could.

Attachment researchers around the world explain that parents do not try to be bad parents. You just learn ineffective relational strategies from your parents, who learned them from their parents, who learned them from their parents, and so on. So, of course, you are going to relate the same way!

As children, we normalize our experiences. Meaning: as a child, everything you experienced was considered "normal," even if your life included many unhealthy characteristics. Children normalize aspects of their lives to be able to cope with difficult situations. For example, a child I was counseling stated, "It is normal that husbands beat their wives." In the same session, he stated, "It is normal to run from the cops." The same child also indicated that he thought it was funny when his dad would punch his mom in the face. He giggled as he shared how he and his brother would laugh. At that point, he had been taken from the home and was living in foster care, separated from his other siblings. To clarify, this was not a sadistic child, but this was his "normal." We all normalize the good, the bad, and the ugly from our childhoods. The older we get, we begin to understand more about what substantiates a broader sense of "normal" as we make friends and visit their homes.

In my own childhood, I remember how my family never took any pain medication when we had headaches. We had two choices: water and sleep. There were times I cried on the couch holding my aching head, but rest was my only hope of relief. I can even normalize and justify it now by saying those experiences taught me how to deal with pain. However, when my children have headaches, I offer them other options when the pain reaches a certain threshold. Take a moment and think back to something you believed was normal as a child. How do you understand it differently now?

As we delve into relationship strategies, connection, and attachment, it will likely stir up some big emotions, which is to be expected, yet I want to share my excitement because you are living in the first generation to fully understand the importance of these factors in your development and, ultimately, your behaviors. We are holding onto the final puzzle piece and setting it on the table to see the finished picture answering why we do what we do. You live in a remarkable time! With this wisdom, we can change so much about the world. As previously mentioned, it begins with you and me taking responsibility for this new information that we have been gifted to impact the world around us. I am so grateful for you and whatever level of commitment you apply to the information contained in this book. I promise it will change you for good.

The first time I really understood attachment theory was at an intensive ten-day training in British Columbia called The Circle of Security®. This model was created by Burt Powell, Kent Hoffman, Glen Cooper, and Bob Marvin. It blew my mind! At that point in my career (and in fatherhood) I, again, thought I had parenting all figured out. This is never a good place to be. Learn from me, we can continuously learn and grow in all areas of life.

During that first training, my mind focused on the ways I was parented and how it shaped my life and my relational strategies. After some intense emotions of my own, I began to see my parents in a different light. The new knowledge allowed me to see them as products of their parents and their parent's parents, etc. Grace and forgiveness filled my heart for the relationship strategies I learned as a child, which were not terrible, just developed from an uninformed perspective due to the lack of understanding of parenting at that time. Like I said, we really have been given a gift in this generation!

A year later I attended a four-day training on the Circle of Security-Parenting® model. Even though I had learned the model, had been teaching other parents the model and had been practicing the model myself, I sat in the second training flooded with more emotions this time about the ways my wife and I still parented our own kids. This was something I did not expect at all. I mean, yes, going into the training I knew I would reevaluate my parenting tactics and the strategies we used for each of our five children, but what I did not expect was to experience intense waves of anger, sadness, and guilt. I was able to forgive myself, just as I had forgiven my parents, but it took the week to sit with the acquired knowledge and refocus on using it to change the future of my parenting. The truth is, no matter how much we beat ourselves up over the past, we change nothing. We only make ourselves miserable and steal the energy we could use for making changes for the future. Guilt is *not* a good motivator.

As you experience this chapter, you will likely have some big emotions of your own on different levels, which is entirely normal and expected. Throughout our journey together, you have practiced witnessing your emotions and thoughts coming up, sitting with them as to not push them away, trying not to give the feelings a label of good or bad, embracing them as part of the gift of living, and then deciding what you want to do with them. Much of the time you have stopped to take deep breaths with Patience.

Hello, Patience.

Every human being on Earth has similar needs to be healthy, as we have discussed: hope, a sense of control, True Self identity, and significance. Also, we all desire to be loved, be accepted, and be safe in a relatively consistent way. In chapter two, we discussed the need of believing you are lovable and acceptable regardless of how you perceive that others love and accept you. We also recognized the need for you to love and accept yourself to be available to love and accept others. In chapter three, Fear, Faith, and Trust emerged as you worked toward the best version of yourself. We also indicated that you have a need for a few transparent relationships in your life. Next, we are going to delve into what secure and insecure attachment looks like and how each influences a person in their relational strategies. This will give you ways to view your strategies and the strategies of others.

Lucky Relational Strategies

Secure attachment is the goal of relationships. In essence, people create containers for others to process, to learn, to heal, and to grow, which is an essential ingredient for an environment conducive for change and Luck. As we discuss the idea of a container, it is not a physical object. The container consists of a space in time combined with emotional openness where you engage in healthy communication with and for another person. Liken the "container" to how Patience provides space for you to process your thoughts and emotions. As previously eluded, you learned how to create secure attachments with others by how you attached to your caregivers. Therefore, the container you create for others in your relationships usually reflects the container your parent's created for you.

In a secure attachment, first, you believe, and you feel loved, accepted, and safe. Attachment research reports that a child needs to experience this at least *thirty percent* of the time to create a secure attachment. Hopefully, this statistic allows you to breathe a sigh of relief if you are a parent. Just like most other things in life, you are not expected to parent perfectly.

What does it look like to know and feel loved? It looks

and feels unconditional.

What does it look like to know and feel accepted? It looks and feels like you are not being judged by your False Self.

What does it look like to know and feel safe? Safety is experienced in multiple ways. You need to feel safe physically; you need to know your body is safe. Every time I allow myself to sit with the statistics for sexual abuse, I feel empty, yet enraged. At the time of writing this book, The National Center for Victims of Crime reports that one out of five girls and one out of twenty boys are sexually abused. Unfortunately, I believe this statistic is likely underreported. To make things worse, family members are culpable for eighty percent of child sexual abuse. As a therapist who has worked directly with the victims of such abuse, I cannot understate the adverse effects of physical and sexual abuse on a person and in their relational strategies, regardless of a caregiver's ability to create a container. There is hope for those of you reading this book who have been on the receiving end of such an abhorrent crime. However, we are all responsible for keeping those around us safe, if it is within our power. To be fair, we are all responsible for keeping ourselves out of danger when possible, as well.

You need to feel safe mentally; you need to believe you are being told the truth regardless of whether you want to hear the truth or not. Interestingly, sometimes we think we are protecting people from hearing the truth because they cannot handle it, but as a rule of thumb, such a strategy does not work well for children or adults. Adults can handle it, but the truth is best received from those in our four and five levels. Kids can handle it when offered in an age-appropriate way from those who have created the container for them. In the end, you want to believe you can trust what someone is saying, which feels safe.

You need to feel safe emotionally; you need to believe that you can expect a consistent range of emotional reaction from someone depending on the situation. For example, if you know you did something that is going to influence someone to be angry, then you can expect a general range of emotional reaction such as expletives, throwing pillows, going for a walk, etc. A problem arises when you receive completely different emotional responses on seperate occasions. This is confusing and leads to never knowing what to expect, which does not feel safe.

You need to feel safe financially; you need to believe that your basic needs of food, water, shelter, and warmth will be met every day without fear. Working with foster children, I have seen kids choose foster parents over their biological parents solely based on financial safety. To the parent, it seems like the child is materialistic. To the child, they want to know they will have a bed to sleep on and food to eat. We may often take for granted that our basic financial needs are being met, but when these needs go unmet for even a short amount of time our brains and bodies panic. Living in panic mode for even a short amount of time can have lasting effects on our behaviors.

Lastly, in marriage, you also need fidelity; you need to believe that your relationship is exclusive, regardless of the problems that arise in the relationship. You need to believe that you can get through everything together, no matter what. You need to have no fear that the other person is going to leave you. The entire next chapter covers communication;

therefore, you will gain more gifts then.

I indicated that the consistency needed to sustain a belief and feeling of love, acceptance, and safety can be estimated at about thirty percent. This is totally doable. To put this into perspective, your goal is to create a *climate* of love, acceptance, and safety, not a single day of weather. Further, Bruce Perry, a psychiatrist who founded the Child Trauma Academy in Texas, reports that consistent, predictable, and repetitive patterns calm the emotional center in the brain called the amygdala. Such patterns calm our brains when they are present in our relationships, as well. Do your best to be consistent, predictable, and repetitive in your connnnections, and you will reap many benefits. You know this for your own life, there are those who say they will be there and those who actually show up. Who in your life has always been there for you no matter what? What has that meant to you?

Do you want to be better at something than someone else? Love them better than they love themselves, show them they are acceptable, create a climate of safety, and then watch the world begin to change!

In addition to creating a container of love, acceptance, and safety, people need to feel autonomous. Meaning, they need to feel like they can be their own person, not smothered. People with secure attachment need to explore alone for their own personal growth. As we age, our exploration looks different, but exploration allows us to feel as though we can handle whatever comes our way. It decreases fear and increases hope, control, responsibility, significance, faith, and self-trust. For some of you, if you are honest with yourselves, you fear exploration, and you actually enjoy being smothered. We will discuss this, as well. Hold tight!

Lastly, when creating a container, in the words of the Circle of Security® model, we all desire to be *welcomed home*. After we learn and grow through our exploration, we desire to be welcomed back and know that we have been missed. Why do you think you look at your phone so frequently? You want to know that someone cares.

Sometimes when you come back home, you are a mess. In being welcomed home, you long to be comforted. If you were physically hurt, then you want someone to help in caring for your wounds. If you were emotionally wounded, you desire to have someone understand what you are experiencing and sit with you while you are hurting. You don't need them to try to fix it or plot revenge. You just need someone to be with you and allow you the space to feel the pain, someone who you know cares for you. If you have ever experienced such a moment, you understand how extraordinary it can be.

Let us put it all together. To create a secure attachment, a child needs to believe and feel that their caregiver is *For Them* by loving them, accepting their True Self, keeping them safe, and offering age-appropriate autonomy. They need to believe that their caregiver is *With Them*, evidenced by welcoming them home, comforting them on their terms, helping them understand their emotions, and helping them cope.

What are the results of secure attachment? First, you learn to create *interdependent* relationships that recognize that all humans are equal; you see that all of our needs are equal; you acknowledge that no one's needs are more important than anyone else's. It becomes clear that getting everyone's needs met, not just our own (yet including our own) is the goal. Interdependent relationships create an environment where you can see your True Self, the potential to trust yourself and others, the ability for self-awareness, and no fear of failure. This leads to honesty, the ability to regulate your own emotions, the capacity to take responsibility, the willingness and the ability to be autonomous, and the potential to fulfill your highest purpose. This mentality further leads to collaboration, growth, innovation, and an opportunity for more needs to be met. Utilizing an interdependent model of relationships, we accept the truth that we do NOT grow if we are not connected. Ultimately, you have Lucky relationships!

Image a tree for a moment. If a branch from the tree has been removed and placed on the ground, then the branch still receives water from the rain and light from the sun, however, because it is not attached to the tree, it withers and dies. Humans are no different. You need connectedness. We all need connectedness. Remember, mind-body-spirit-connection!

UnLucky Relational Strategies

Three relational strategies fail to create secure attachment or connectedness. Again, if you notice some emotional reactions coming up just witness them, sit with them, do your best not to judge them, and then decide if you want to do something with the emotions. At this juncture, it can be helpful to reiterate that parents do not intentionally try to create insecure attachments. All parents are trying to do the best they can for their children, in the best way they know how, and with the resources they possess.

At first, an *independent* strategy in relationships looks as though a person does not need other people to function or be happy, which is a protective defense strategy created to fight against the pain of not being comforted or welcomed home as a child. This person has cut themselves off from their feelings by telling themselves that they do not need anyone. The way they comfort themselves or self-soothe is through performance techniques that can look like constant cleaning, exercising, or some other form of organizing the world around them to deal with the disorganization within. They never felt or believed they were loved or accepted for their True Self. This False Self focus leads them to strive for perfect behavior because, as a child, that was the only way to keep their parents happy and if their parents became unhappy, then they were unhappy. As children, they could not handle feeling unhappy because their parents did not help them appropriately manage their emotions. Therefore, they would try even harder to be perfect.

A child who has learned an independent relational strategy often becomes a parent with the picture-perfect family because their relational strategy has been passed down to their kids. The parent pushes their kids to do activities, just like they do (and did), and it appears like they can never sit down, often due to feeling as though stopping to rest equates to laziness. When anyone asks them for comfort (which they never received and don't know how to offer), they get anxious or angry. They may exhibit behaviors such as laughing at the one asking for comfort, yelling at them, telling them to suck it up, or pushing them to play with a toy or do another activity to allow the child to sooth himself or herself.

To break it down, an independent strategy creates a

lack of connectedness because those using this strategy are emotionally unavailable, cannot trust anyone else, fear failure, hyper-focus on perfect behavior or the False Self, frequently judge themselves and others, often become anxious or angry when asked for comfort (or when attempting to self-soothe through activities), and find it hard to authentically connect with others. But, of course, they would be like this! They learned this pattern from a caregiver who learned it from a caregiver, etc.

Second, a *dependent* relational strategy appears as a person in constant need of attention, comfort, or praise due to the fear that those around them are going to leave them, abandon them, or never come back. Dependent relational strategies act as a protective defense that was created in childhood when the person was not allowed to explore or experience a high level of autonomy, even when the person was welcomed home or comforted as a child it was on the caregiver's terms. The caregiver created an environment focused on using the child to meet their own emotional needs, but only until they didn't need the child, regardless of whether the child still needed comfort. When the child attempted to explore and gain autonomy, the caregiver felt alone, feared abandonment, and needed comfort for themselves, therefore, they forced the child to stop exploring to meet their own emotional needs. However, when the child agreed to stop exploring and looked for a welcome home, the caregiver felt overwhelmed and pushed them away, which communicated, "I'm here, but I'm not here." Everything was on the caregiver's terms, which left the child striving to be good enough for their caregiver. Eventually, the child decided it was best not to explore, which created an over-reliance on others, and feelings of abandonment when alone.

A child who has learned a dependent relational strategy often becomes an adult who is emotionally overly needy, lacks the ability to self-soothe, cannot trust himself/herself, can only rely on others, fears failure, experiences little to no autonomy, fears being alone, struggles with being honest with people due to the fear that they will say or do the wrong thing, and focuses on being "good enough" through the False Self. If you find yourself identifying with this relational strategy, you may be feeling shame, anger, sadness, or a host of many other feelings right now. But, of course, anyone could turn out this way if they were raised by parents who experienced the same pattern.

The last relational strategy is called *disorganized*. The majority of children who you see with outrageous behaviors are experiencing a disorganized relational strategy in their homes. A child's caregiver is both the most significant source of fear and the person they want the most because they want and need to feel safe. The child needs the caregiver, but cannot trust the caregiver because the caregiver is not safe. The caregiver exhibits one or more parenting strategies at any given time, but all of them result in the child not feeling safe including being physically, verbally, or disciplinarily *mean*; coming across as physically or emotionally *weak* or not being able to manage their child's life; being physically or emotionally *gone* and not interacting with the child. The caregivers never learned how to create a structure to help the child organize their own emotions or behaviors. Putting trauma aside, disorganized relational strategies create the perfect storm for adult personality disorders.

A child who has learned a disorganized relational

strategy often becomes an adult who, understandably, does not feel safe, loved, or accepted. As a result, they struggle with trusting themselves or others, they fear abandonment, they have little to no ability to self-soothe or allow others to soothe them, they present with uncontrollable behavior issues, they feel incapable of autonomy or taking responsibility for themselves, they struggle with being honest, and their False Self is all they know.

You may find it easy to pinpoint those in your world operating with a disorganized relational strategy (especially children) and to point the finger at the parent blaming them for their poor parenting style. However, as you are beginning to understand, they learned it from their parents who learned it from their parents. Just like the futility of asking someone who has no hammer to build a house, believing someone should know a different way of parenting from their parents is futile. Instead of blaming, I am asking for empathy. Blaming gets them (and us) nowhere. Empathy is the only way you can create an environment where you may be able to offer them a hammer and teach them how to build the house. As you work toward the goal of interdependence, recognize that the goal is for *everyone* to get their needs met, regardless of the family into which they were born. Let us set aside blame because it is a useless tool, and it leads only to destruction.

A moment with Patience is definitely needed.

Hello, Patience.

Other Connection Considerations

As we look at relational strategies in the home to

understand our own relational strategies and the strategies we see in the world around us, it helps to be aware that when two people get married, they each bring in their own relational strategies. This leads to a period of adjustment in the first several years of marriage and, unfortunately, has led to a high number of divorces. We reviewed four strategies: interdependent, independent, dependent, and disorganized, which leads to a combination of ten possibilities in marriage: interdependent-interdependent, interdependent-independent, interdependent-dependent, interdependent-disorganized, independent-independent, independent-dependent, independent-disorganized, dependent-dependent, dependent-disorganized, and disorganized-disorganized. Whole books have been written on relational strategies in marriage; therefore we are not going to discuss the intricacies of each pair. However, knowing what you now know, it may be helpful to identify your parents' relational strategies. Notice your personal, relational strategy as a result of the combination of strategies in your home growing up. If you are married, can you determine your spouse's relational strategy or that of their parents? If you have children, identify the strategies they have learned as a result of the combination of your own and your spouse's relational strategies. Lastly, if your children are dating or married, note the strategy type they tend to gravitate toward.

Understanding relational strategies benefits you, your marriage, your home, and the health of all of your purpose-driven future endeavors. Healthy family units are foundational in creating healthy, thriving communities. Communities make up states, states make up countries, and countries make up the world. Without healthy family units, the world will gravitate toward chaos. As we have discussed over and over, a movement of change all starts with *you*.

The cycle of relational strategies often repeats itself from generation to generation, through caregiver to caregiver, and from parent to child. It will continue until one person begins learning from their past and trying a new strategy. You can be the person to break the chain in your family, which can change the course of many generations to come. Both power and responsibility flow from acknowledging this truth. Please remember, you do not have to do it alone, nor do you have to do it perfectly. Allow this opportunity to offer you a sense of personal control, which can lead to an intense amount of hope. Embrace it. Own it! Be Lucky!

To complete our discussion of connectedness, it is imperative that you understand what you can do with this new information. I asked you to recognize your own relational strategy for you to grow toward interdependence. Recognizing your great strength and influence through your relationships with others can lead you to begin modeling interdependence with others, which creates the container conducive for change and being Lucky. Four questions can help guide you in understanding if you are creating the container for others:

1. Can they be autonomous and still feel loved by you?
2. Can they be their True Selves and still feel accepted by you?
3. Can they trust you to be safe?
4. Are you acting these ways out relatively consistently?

Before beginning this book, did you recognize and accept the far-reaching power and influence that resides within you? How would your life be different if you unleashed that power? What would happen to you, your family, and your community? Sit with that energy and emotion as it wells up inside right now. Let go of any inhibitions you have with every exhale. Close your eyes and envision the future impact of your personal, relational changes. Draw it out or paint it, if you like. Write a song or poem about how different the future will be.

What will *you* do? Who will you be? Take a moment and write your answer down. Tell someone today about your vision. Your Lucky future starts now!

The Gift of Luck Stages of Change

Connectedness through interdependence.
Fearless Purpose. Truth, Trusting, Faith, and Risk.
True Self Identity. Self-Love and Self-Acceptance.
Hope. Control. Self-responsibility. Priorities.

6

Crafting glasses

Growing up in northeastern Ohio, the electricity in the house seemed to go out at least once every couple of months, if not more often, due to storms or car accidents. For whatever reason, the outages seemed to happen the majority of the time after sunset. As a result, my family and I would be fumbling around at home in the dark, trying to locate a flashlight. Inevitably, the flashlight was never in the place where it was supposed to be. This left us using matches and candles as our source of light. All seven people in the house would gather around the person who found the source of light as they led the way around the house.

Attempting to use all the information from this book to be Lucky, impact the world around you, and bring about change while practicing poor communication skills is as ineffective as walking around in the dark without a source of light. The way you communicate all of the knowledge and wisdom you have gained throughout experiencing *The Gift of Luck* enables you to be a source of light to the world. For this reason, this chapter is dedicated to giving you the tools to be as bright a light as possible to the world, with the ability to draw people close and lead them to change for good. Be the light!

The question to answer in this chapter: What kind of glasses are you crafting? Imagine that you are handing out glasses for people to see you and the world with every interaction you have. Kent Hoffman said it best: you don't see the world the way it is, you see it the way you are. From birth, your belief system is molded by the interactions you have with those around you, and this is how you view the world. Another way to ask the same question: how are you teaching people to experience you through your communication? Use these questions and understanding as the compass to direct you through this chapter.

Communication Breakdown

As you have now come to understand the importance of connectedness, recognize that communication acts as the food or sustenance for connectedness. Without effective communication, the relationship will inevitably experience failure to thrive. Even if you agree with and believe the tenets of interdependence, but lack the tools or ability to be able to communicate love, acceptance, and safety, then your capacity to influence powerfully will be diminished, decreasing your capability to be Lucky. Your light will be very dim, and people will look for a brighter source of light elsewhere, even if those sources are unhealthy or are hurting them. Continue to invest in your future self and those around you by taking this chapter seriously and learning to grow in your communication skills. Work at crafting glasses of love, acceptance, and safety to feed the relationships around you.

After a couple of twists and turns in college, ultimately, I chose interpersonal and public communication for an undergraduate degree (in addition to business) mainly because I wanted to be able to communicate effectively with those around me and from a stage. My professors drilled into my head the importance of communication, as well as the variety of ways we are actually communicating. The first and most crucial fact about communication you need to understand and to accept is that only seven percent of what you are communicating consists of the words you speak. Reread that sentence. Yes, this is accurate. Only seven percent of communication is based on the actual words you speak.

I cannot think of a better way to illustrate this point in our technological world than to discuss texting. Do the meaning of your texts ever become misconstrued and taken in some other way than you were trying to communicate? When you have been attempting to be funny while texting with someone from work and they are not familiar with your sense of humor, you can come across in a myriad of ways, many of which can create extreme awkwardness afterwards. As a result, we now use emojis in our texts to show our emotions as a way to more clearly communicate the meaning of our written words. The main point is that words give us an additional vehicle to interact with others, but the depth of meaning found in our communication happens primarily beyond the words we speak.

Second, thirty-eight percent of the meaning of your communication comes through *how* you say the words. This includes your tone of voice, intonation, pitch, volume, speed, hesitation, pausing, rhythm, and even dialect. Think of the difference between an actor/actress who you would consider good at what they do. Now think of an actor/actress who has much more to learn. An actor can say all the right lines, but not be able to clearly communicate what the director wants in a moment, and it makes all the difference as to whether you continue watching or whether you quickly redirect your attention to something else. The director may have a fascinating story to tell, yet no one will hear it.

The most influential aspect of communication, delivering fifty-five percent of your message, is demonstrated through body language. Body language includes facial expressions, eye movement, eye contact, head movement, posture, gestures, proximity, touch, dress, and artifacts (i.e., a clipboard, a stethoscope, or a wedding ring). Do you remember when you were a child, and your caregiver gave you "the look?" From just a glance, you knew something terrible was coming if you did not stop doing what you were doing right away. Or, consider the importance of a handshake. What does a moderately firm handshake communicate compared to a limp-fish handshake? How does gender play into the meaning of the handshake?

Culture plays a large part in dictating the meaning of each of these body language expressions. For example, in the United States, our personal bubble is wider than those in many other countries. If someone accustomed to speaking socially within eighteen inches of someone else in their culture approaches you at that distance when you are used to eighteen inches as a distance meant for intimacy and not a social distance, it creates awkwardness. You might not even be able to focus on the words they are saying; you will likely just try to break free of their uncomfortable up-close and personal distance. What does this communicate to them?

Another vital aspect of connection through communication to consider is that you are communicating when you are not even present with a person. This clearly reveals your priorities, trustworthiness, authenticity, love, etc. These aspects of communication are best demonstrated and not spoken. Ultimately, these demonstrations craft the glasses through which each person sees you. The glasses you craft for others alters their perspective of every verbal and nonverbal communication you have with them after that.

Consider how you communicate what is valuable in your life by the amount of time you give it, the duration of time you think about it, the frequency of time you talk about it, and the amount of energy you exert toward it. Many of the messages you send may be unintentional due to a lack of awareness. However your spouse, children, family, and co-workers are picking up on them. Conversely, think of a moment when having someone just show up in your time of need. What did that mean to you? Likely, volumes were communicated by such an act. Let it be priority number one to give those around you a proper set of glasses.

Whether you realize it or not, even silence can be more articulate than words at times. As a child, my brothers would give me the silent treatment when they were mad at me, which was the worst form of punishment because it communicated that I did not even exist to them. They pretended for what seemed like *hours* that my presence was a result of the wind. I've since forgiven them, but I'm still working on forgiving them for the Chinese torture techniques. On a more serious note, think about what happens when you give another person the therapeutic silent space and time to just be with them at the moment. This communicates that you accept them where they are, without fear, and without needing them to be fixed. This is very powerful for both people involved.

Like it or not, you never cease communicating with those around you. Do you see the need to spend an entire chapter discussing all of this?

To adequately cover communication, we will begin by delving into verbal communication and then nonverbal communication. Even though nonverbal communication communicates meaning more clearly and loudly, verbal communication dramatically enhances the impact you can make on those in your world. Just like in poetry, books, or song, our words do matter even if they are only seven percent of what we communicate.

Communication Styles

Four main verbal communication styles exist including passive, aggressive, passive-aggressive, and assertive. Each has a belief system from which it stems. Each style is expressed as a result of the influences of interactions and glasses a person has been given from their caregivers and those around them.

Passive

Underlying a passive style of communication is the belief that everyone else's needs are more important than your own. A one-word label for someone using passivity as their primary form of communication is "doormat." Unfortunately, people practicing a passive communication style continue to get taken advantage of while trying to please others, and often times attempt to gain acceptance through their acts of generosity. Often, the result is a person with low self-esteem. They bend over backwards by saying yes to everyone, but since no one person can actually follow through when saying yes to *everyone* they do not always follow through on what they say they will do, therefore, people do not respect them or their yes. Others view them as wishy-washy and unreliable. If, on the off chance that they are trustworthy with their yes, they likely feel overwhelmed all the time and their family relationships may be suffering. Their relational strategy is often dependent, and all of their efforts are an attempt to feel loved and accepted by others. Conflict resolution often occurs by either accommodating everyone else's needs or merely avoiding conflict all together. When conflict is not appropriately addressed and resolved, little to no growth is experienced in the relationship, and it is never given the opportunity to mature.

Aggressive

The belief that my needs are more important than everyone else's needs leads to the second verbal communication style: aggressive. A bully embodies aggressiveness by working toward getting only his own needs met regardless of how many people are hurt as a result. This style of communication often leads to a situation where the bully does not have any real friends. The cronies that surround him are only friends with him so that they are not the target of the aggressiveness, but in the end, relationships fail due to the person's selfishness. They are left alone, yet again, even though much of their efforts are created as a way to feel safe. It is easy to see a commonality to an independent relational strategy. Aggressiveness often leads to a competition style of conflict resolution, which is a win-at-all-costs approach. The problem with having to always be right or win all the time is that it leads to relationship loss. Any time one person wins, and another loses, the relationship loses. No emotional connection growth occurs, only bitterness and resentment.

Passive-Aggressive

The third style is a combination of passivity and aggressiveness. Often, passivity is practiced in front of others while aggressiveness is exhibited after one walks away. Someone who lives out a passive-aggressive style of communication has cycles of explosions. They can only take acting like the doormat for so long before they explode at others. Unfortunately, spouses and children get the brunt of the aggressiveness because they are close targets and younger children usually can't retaliate. As a result, people practicing passive-aggressive communication receive a combination of the negative aspects of both passivity and aggressiveness. People avoid them, their self-esteem is low, and they feel lonely due to few, if any, real friends.

Another common expression of passive-aggressive communication is sarcasm. Early on in my marriage, my wife and I were told that sarcasm has no place in a marriage. In truth, sarcasm has no place in any healthy relationship. At the end of the day, sarcasm opens the door to say something truthful to hurt others while passing it off as a joke. I have talked to many couples who declare that sarcasm works in their relationship. Personally, I think these couples will eventually see the devastation that has been caused by the sarcasm, hopefully, before it is too late. In summary, relationships do not thrive utilizing either passive, aggressive, or passive-aggressive styles of communication.

Assertiveness

Assertiveness results from the same belief system as those who connect through interdependence: everyone's needs are equal and they want everyone to get their needs met including themselves. Relationships hold the highest importance, especially over having to be right. People who practice assertiveness are able to say "no" when necessary to balance getting their own needs met while following through when they say "yes." Others respect them, their self-esteem is healthy, and they can build thriving relationships with others because they have no fear of abandonment. Collaboration is their conflict resolution style where each person speaks their needs about the situation, followed by both creating a strategy to meet each individual's needs. In this model of conflict resolution both feel as though they win; therefore, the relationship prevails and emotional connection flourishes. Ultimately, practicing assertiveness allows a person to feel and be authentic with themselves and others. People crave authenticity in others, just as you do.

You may find that you practice each of these styles of communication in different settings or with different people. At work you may find it easy to practice assertiveness while being passive with your spouse, and aggressive with your children or sales people. Allow yourself to be honest with yourself, without judgment, recognizing the strategies and communication styles you use as you go through your day. When you notice a pattern of relationship-limiting communication, then you have the option of changing it. If you are willing to be more proactive, take a moment right now to assess when and with whom you practice passivity, aggressiveness, and passive-aggressiveness to build a change plan. Remember, however, that each communication style begins with a belief system and all the other factors of change we have talked about up to this point. This process is cumulative in nature, and no one aspect can be overlooked when attempting to make changes in your life.

A great time to meet with Patience.

Hello, Patience.

Putting Assertiveness into Practice

After reading about communication and conflict resolution styles, it may seem easy to pinpoint a potential growth area for yourself. As I worked through the process of refining my own communication, I learned that the first best step was to remember: when in doubt, listen. Often times our initial reaction to relational conflict is to begin talking by sharing how the other person wronged us or how we have an unmet need. What does this sound like? Yep, blame. What does blame do? It gives away power, which decreases hope. If you focus on what you have control over, which is you, then you have so much more potential for assertiveness and collaboration.

Step one is to listen more. As you are listening, attempt

to seek understanding. This communicates empathy while you gain a greater perspective of the situation. Curiously ask clarifying questions when things don't make sense. Most people do not intentionally try to hurt others. If you can get to the point of believing that most people have good intentions, then empathy flows more naturally within yourself and in your relationships. As you model empathy, you craft glasses tinted with love and acceptance for others.

A clear distinction needs to be made at this point between empathy and sympathy. Imagine yourself walking along down a road in your own journey toward the best version of yourself, and you hear something. As you stop and listen, you recognize the sound of someone in distress coming from ahead. The voice gets louder as you begin to walk at a quicker pace. Soon you have located the person belonging to the sound, and they are down in a pit struggling to get out. You ask what happened, and they begin telling you a story that evidently evokes much emotion within them evidenced by the anger and free-flowing tears down their cheeks. At this point, they have not asked for help even though you can tell they are miserable in the pit.

You have two options at this point: empathy or sympathy. Sympathy would look like you climbing down into the pit, which would drudge up a host of emotions within you (whether the emotions are from past hurts you have experienced or even if they are just taking on the emotions being felt by the person in the pit). Here is the problem: when you climb into the pit with the person, take on their emotions, and allow your own emotional past to surface, then you are both stuck in the pit without a way to get out.

The other option is empathy. Empathy allows you to

stay at the surface where you can hear the story clearly enough without being engulfed by the seeming hopelessness pouring out from within the pit. You can understand what the other person is thinking, feeling, and going through without having to take the burden on as your own, which would eventually lead to burnout and potentially enabling.

After you believe you understand the thoughts and the emotional state of the other person in their situation, attempt to share a snapshot or "brief picture" to them through *reflection*. Reflection is practiced by paraphrasing what you heard the other person express they are thinking and feeling in their situation without saying it in the exact same words.

A simple way to start reflecting is by beginning the sentence with *"so what I hear you saying is..."* As you communicate what you heard, the other person often resounds with an emphatic *"Yes!"* or they will correct you by telling you more. Either way, you are communicating that you love them and accept them enough to really listen to them. As you know from personal experience, being heard feels like such a gift in a world where few take the time to slow down and truly listen. David W. Augsburger in his book *Caring Enough to Hear and Be Heard* stated, "Being heard is so close to being loved that for the average person, they are almost indistinguishable." This is a perfect way to build those glasses.

Once basic reflection becomes more natural, then you can listen for meaning. For example, imagine your spouse angrily approaches you and discusses how you left the towel on the floor in the bathroom...again! It would be easy to get defensive, angry, and begin justifying it as a mistake. But that was the old version of you before reflection, right?! Instead you recognize that the meaning behind the anger has to do with how your spouse works hard to keep the house clean, and it feels like you don't appreciate what your spouse does when you carelessly leave your towel on the floor in the bathroom (when they have asked you over and over to hang it up). If you reflected back a version of that with an apology, then your spouse will feel heard, understood, and valued. The conflict that could have been much worse turned into an opportunity to draw the two of you closer as a team. This is a big difference! Of course, making it a priority to consistently pick up the towel to *demonstrate* you value your spouse and the work they do will further connect the two of you.

Consider this example of listening for meaning. When I get home, my wife and I spend ten minutes sharing with one another the happenings of each of our days. Perhaps she shares that our kids did not help in the way she needed, one of the sprinklers broke again, she found aphids in the kale, and she noticed the truck was leaking oil on the driveway. I could reflect, "That sounds like a really frustrating day! That is way more unexpected things happening in one day than normal." In this example, notice how I did not have to rehash everything she said she went through, nor did I attempt to give advice on how to fix it or offer to fix anything at this point. I just listened and reflected.

Advice giving and trying to fix things before listening and reflecting makes the situation about *you*. Even if the conversation is directed *at* you, at this point in the discussion, it is not *about* you. All your person needs at that moment is for you to be with them, listen from the top of the pit, attempt to understand what is going on in their pit, and communicate back to them, "I'm here. I care. I understand," through your reflection. Once they feel heard, then you wait to see if they even want you to give advice or fix anything.

The vast majority of the time, people do not want to be fixed. If it is significant to the other person, they will ask you to help them after they believe you understand the situation. Another option is asking if they want you to do something after you can tell they feel heard. Coming back to the scenario of my wife's frustrating day, I could have offered to discipline the kids, fix the sprinkler head, kill the aphids or make a call to get the truck into the shop. If I would have offered to do any of that before listening and reflecting I would never have found out that she already did three of the four things. After being heard, my wife probably would ask for me to call to get the truck in or I would ask if she would like me to take care of it. A situation that could have potentially pushed us apart resulted, again, in drawing us closer as a team.

One last tip for crafting glasses of empathy. It can be extremely beneficial as when you attempt to seek understanding from another person to avoid "Why" questions. For example, *"Why did you do that?"* or *"Why would you think that?"* "Why" questions feel like an attack. What happens when you are attacked? You get defensive, of course! You get the boxing gloves on and ready yourself for another knockdown, drag out fight. At that point, it can *feel* like you are against them, as opposed to the truth, which is that in every conflict it is the two of you against the problem. Do not miss this: when working toward interdependence, every situation requires a team effort against the issue. No person is the problem. People are not problems. People's behaviors can be problematic, but that is not their True Self. Do your best not to focus on your False Self or the False Self of others. We have already discussed the ramifications of that, and the outlook is lousy.

Now that you understand listening, empathy, and reflection, you are ready to be assertive because, without the first three components, the former rarely is successfully carried out. However, when teaching people about communication, assertiveness is often practiced before listening, empathy, and reflection. I cannot tell you how many times I hear, *"I calmly put my foot down, but it did not turn out how I thought it would."* Assertiveness is fourth in line! In conflict resolution, a reflection can help to draw out what the other person's needs are in the situation, which is crucial when working toward interdependence. Once the other person's needs are identified and reflected, then your needs can be expressed to find a collaborative strategy that will meet both your needs and their needs because, again, the goal of practicing interdependence is to meet the needs of both people, whenever possible.

Another tip about practicing assertiveness. Just as with empathy, the critical nature of semantics cannot be underestimated. Avoiding "You" statements when attempting to communicate empathy will help decrease defensiveness in the other person. For example, *"You did not say I love you back to me, which hurt really bad, and that is why I left."* What does this sound like? Yep, blame, again. But, it also seems like an attack.

Regardless of how the other person behaves, you are responsible for your thoughts, emotions, and behaviors. Remember, no one can *make* you feel anything; *you* react to the situation. *You* are in control over you. As a way to keep yourself in check, think of assertiveness as speaking Truth in

Love. Therefore, another way to say this could be, *"I felt hurt when I did not hear an 'I love you' in return, so I left."* It still helps the other person to understand your reaction while taking ownership of your own actions and ending the blame game.

With children, teenagers, and adults alike it can help to share your intentions before being assertive and speaking the truth in love by stating, *"I want what is best for you, for me, and this relationship."* If your spouse prefaced a discussion with this statement, what would that communicate to you and how might this affect your responses? Speaking honestly and giving honest feedback are both aspects of assertiveness. When uttered with pure intentions to deliver truth in love, you are doing the best you can, which is all anyone could ever ask of you.

Lastly, remember that conflict is not bad in and of itself. Conflict creates an opportunity for growth. You will never change or grow in your relationships without healthy conflict resolution practice. Think of conflict like going to the dentist. The experience is rarely pleasant when you are in the chair, but when you leave the office the pain is gone, and you are better off than when you went in. Conflict increases emotional connection and draws people closer together when it is resolved.

This is the perfect spot for some deep breaths.

Hello, Patience.

Creating the Container

The last chapter concluded that everyone in the world has a need to know someone is For Them and With Them. How do we communicate that? What does it look like? Notice that I didn't ask, "What does that *sound* like?" By now you understand more of the reasons why. Ninety-three percent of what we communicate happens beyond the words we speak. To show anyone you care about them and that you are For Them, it looks seeking understanding (empathy), speaking truth in love (assertiveness), striving to have all needs met for both in the relationship (interdependence), and healthy conflict resolution where win-win strategies are created together (collaboration).

Further, we discussed being aware of *how* you say something and what your body language looks like while saying it dramatically influences the meaning you are communicating. Consider a pointed finger as opposed to an open hand facing upward. Which communicates blame and which communicates I am For You? Of course, this is why our parents told us not to point fingers at people. You are expressing something you may not have intended to communicate with that finger. The tone of voice and body language takes time and practice to change, but it is not impossible. If you genuinely plan to show someone you are For Them, then your motivation will be high, and you will be more intentional with your non-verbal communication.

One other aspect of being For Them is doing your best to keep yourself and others safe by getting rid of blame and sarcasm. These communicate that you are For Yourself. Also, you can communicate that you are For Them and for their safety by going to bat for them. When someone else treats them poorly, step up and say something. Think back to a time when someone stood up for you. What did that communicate to you?

How do you show someone you are With Them?

Showing up consistently and authentically while communicating that you love them and accept them regardless of their behaviors clearly demonstrates that you are With Them. Can it help to verbalize your intentions? Absolutely! However, as we have discussed, words only go as far as the glasses you have given them.

A question always arises when discussing being For and With. *How do I know when I am helping or enabling?* Motivation is a crucial factor when answering this question. Not their motivation, but yours. Answering this question for yourself: whose needs are you trying to meet? Are you trying to meet your own need to be needed or are you attempting to be With Them through their change story? One way to help understand the difference is by realizing that enabling is doing something for someone that they can do for themselves. Being With Them at that moment looks like being beside them while *they* do it. Remember, when you do things for them that they can do, this results in stripping them of their control, power, hope, and autonomy. Show that you believe in them by being beside them while they do it. It may not be what they *want* at that moment, but I can assure you that it is what they *need*.

Deciding whether a person can actually do something can be extremely difficult, especially when it comes to mental health issues and trauma. It can be difficult to fully understand when you have never lived with anxiety and depression or lived through traumatic experiences, but all three can be debilitating at times. Something that may not seem traumatic to you can be very traumatic to someone else, depending on many factors that will be discussed in the next chapter. If you are having trouble deciding if you are helping or enabling then seek out professional help.

On the other hand, each person has the responsibility to seek out help and work to overcome challenges as best they can for themselves. This process may look different from how you think it should be. If you or someone you know is not progressing in these areas, then where do you start to look? Hope. Yes, revisit chapter one.

As a last thought, I want you to think about what happens within you when you do not receive the message that someone is For You and With You. We end up not seeing things as they are, we end up seeing things as *we* are. When we do not feel like others love us, then we assume the worst in their communication with us. As I said before, the vast majority of people do not want to be hurtful. If you are not feeling like people are For You, and With You, then this is the best time for you to reassess your communication skills. We both know that you have no direct control over changing the way others communicate with you, but I do know that you have control over reassessing your own communication style, as well as, teaching others how to converse with you. What kind of glasses are you handing out? Remember, you are unceasingly communicating with others, and they have learned how to interact with you by the boundaries that you have or have not set, and the ways by which you demonstrate that you are For Them and With Them.

I have no doubt that you have had someone in mind while reading this entire chapter. Take a moment right now, close your eyes and picture this person in as much detail as you can, even to the point of being able to smell them. Play out the communication change or changes you want to make. Who do you want to be? Notice how they react. Witness how your feelings change as the imaginary tether of the relationship draws you closer to each other. That's right. You have just made the first step in crafting new glasses for them.

Simply put, you need others to be to be Lucky. You cannot thrive disconnected from a community of people. Without being able to communicate healthily, Luck will only be something you see in others. What will you try differently in your communication today? Who will be your first recipient? If this will be a dynamic change of connecting, then make sure to have the oxygen tank ready when they have a heart attack. Go get 'em!

Communicating empathy, assertiveness, and collaboration.
Connectedness through interdependence.
Fear versus Faith/Trust. Purpose.
Fearless Purpose. Truth, Trusting, Faith, and Risk.
True Self Identity. Self-Love and Self-Acceptance.

7

A bit of science

From the day I was born, my life has been influenced by the effects of my birth defect. It has altered my entire belief system, which has affected the way I eat, the people I relate to, the places I frequent, my activities, and on and on. Not only has it changed *my* life, but it has also affected the lives of those around me. If my body would have developed normally, my mom may not have ever sought out alternative medicine or started an alternative clinic or health food store. My siblings and I may not have ever pursued careers in the helping professions. This goes to show that even though our bodies do not give us value or define us, our bodies do influence many aspects of our lives, including motivation and change. Another essential element of discussing our bodies in regard to motivation is that they allow us to build understanding and, hopefully, empathy for ourselves and for others, which (as we discussed in the last chapter) draws us deeper into interconnectedness and being Lucky.

Lucky Brain

Primitive, Limbic, Cortex, oh my!

To understand Luck and change in a transformative way, you have to be informally introduced to the brain, to some of its specific functions, and to how it relates to your body, to your behavior, and, ultimately, to your motivation to change. This is your Lucky brain!

You have biological needs that supersede all higher-order thinking, which makes it extremely difficult to do anything other than attempt to meet your physiological needs when they are unmet. One curious aspect about your brain is the way it perceives your needs. Whether you have a real need, a perceived need, or even an imagined need, your brain gives that particular need precedence over all other things in your world (especially concerning your biological needs and safety needs). For example, if you have a migraine or some other kind of intense pain, then you are going to have a hard time concentrating on anything other than the pain. It is possible yet difficult.

Dr. Bruce Perry developed a model that has become more and more accepted in scientific circles called the neurosequential model of development. I attended an all-day lecture that changed my life by helping me reframe everything I already knew about our brains. The new information gave me a framework I will now share with you. His model posits that our brain develops in a sequence. To help make it easier to understand, he breaks the brain down into three main areas in regards to function: the primitive brain, the limbic system, and the cortex.

The primitive brain includes the parts of the brain that all animals have because they control many involuntary basic functions including breathing, digesting food, body temperature, heart rate, blood pressure, and receiving input from the primary senses (among other vital activities). As you may notice, many of these functions have a rhythmic pattern to them that is essential to your body's success. Notice your body right now. Connect with your breathing. Place your hand on your heart and feel the patterned beat and pulse. If you have recently eaten, you may even feel how your digestion has a rhythm as peristalsis takes your food through the intestines. There is a consistency in the rhythms just as there is consistency in your body temperature and blood pressure.

Dr. Perry determined that consistent, repetitive, and predictable rhythms and patterns are crucial to the success of the primitive brain and to the healing of the primitive brain. Music, walking, running, dancing, jumping, and so many other consistent, repetitive, and predictable patterned activities in your life help to release the primitive brain of the stress, trauma, and negative energy stored in the body. This is the reason movement, as opposed to a sedentary lifestyle, promotes health. Movement allows your body to build endurance, burn off toxicity, and release emotionally toxic energy to keep your body healthy and thriving.

The limbic system, or as many call it the "emotion station," allows you to regulate your emotions. Sometimes the limbic system takes over to keep you safe by fighting or fleeing while other times you just freeze or disassociate. Which do you tend to gravitate toward when experiencing a scary situation?

Interestingly, attachment and connection also process in the limbic system, which explains why connection with others helps in your emotional regulation. Relationship allows this area of the brain to heal. When you are feeling overwhelmed, frustrated, angry, or some other big emotion, do you have someone you can go to who just seems to calm you down by merely being around them? Or maybe you are that calming force that other people come to when they are dysregulated. This speaks volumes about who you are, however, it is imperative for your brain's sake to have someone whom you can go to, as well. As Dr. Perry stated, "The brain is fundamentally a social organ," which makes us relational beings. We need each other.

Your cognitive brain (or cortex), which differentiates humans from all other animals, is the layer of the brain a few millimeters thick covering the rest of the brain. The cortex allows you to think, to reason, and to have consciousness. We will spend a whole chapter discussing the cognitive brain and the importance of your belief system and mindset in chapter nine. For now, understand that just as consistent, predictable, and repetitive patterns calm and heal the primitive brain and connection calms and helps heal the limbic system, you can change the course of your life by the way you think. It has been said many ways through history. Proverbs 23:7 states, "As a man thinketh in his heart, so he is." Rene Descartes wrote, "I think; therefore, I am." In current culture, psychologists, therapists, and lay people have written volumes of books on how to change your mindset. Why? Because it is true.

Developmental Healing

Beyond the main three areas of the brain, let us briefly

look at brain development. Dr. Perry calls his model *neurosequential* to indicate that your brain developed in the womb sequentially, or in a particular order, as you were being formed. It continues to develop sequentially in the way it functions, as well. The primitive brain matures in the womb to take care of all the involuntary bodily functioning. However, the outside environment can affect its development and operation. Whereas, the limbic system and cortex mature after birth. Children need assistance developing their limbic system by helping them understand their emotions, in addition to learning healthy connections through modeling as described in the last chapter. The cortex develops at different rates, but by the age of approximately twenty-five years old, your cortex matures fully. When you think about a teenager and their decision making skills, it makes sense that their cortex is not fully developed yet. Therefore, their immaturity is not entirely their fault.

No brain handles life the exact same way, and traumatic experiences stifle the brain's development. If you have experienced multiple adverse childhood experiences (ACEs) including emotional, physical, or sexual abuse, emotional or physical neglect, domestic violence, household substance abuse, household mental illness, parental separation or divorce, or family member incarceration, then your brain development has been affected. The more ACEs you experienced (especially in your formative years), the more your brain needs movement, connection, and cognitive restructuring to heal.

The way our brains develop directly affects the way we act. Abraham Maslow created a model called the hierarchy of needs showing that animals and humans meet their biological needs of finding food, water, sex, and shelter (which corresponds to the activity in the primitive brain) before all other needs. For example, if you are starving or dehydrated, you will focus on nothing else until those basic needs are met. Next, the brain focuses on regulating the basic functions of the body, while the higher functioning areas of the brain (especially the cortex) become harder to access. Think about what happens when you are starving. Your hunger greatly influences your emotions, your behavior, the way you relate to others, your heart rate, blood pressure, and body temperature. Do you see the connection? Coming back to the ACEs, it is likely that anyone who lived through adverse childhood experiences probably had a lower stress tolerance than most (primitive brain), had a difficult time making friends (limbic brain), and struggled to concentrate, memorize, and learn in school (cognitive brain), all of which can significantly affect bodily health for the rest of one's life. Our brain development is directly influenced by our experiences.

There is hope! Neurologists used to believe that the brain damage from trauma could not heal due to the inability to create new neurons or nerve cells. At the beginning of this century, research exploded in the areas of neurogenesis and neuroplasticity disproving the old way of thinking. Our brains can heal and grow. This is great news!

Research has also indicated that just as the brain develops sequentially, the brain heals in sequence, as well. To heal your brain, start by practicing consistent, predictable, and repetitive patterns daily to heal the primitive brain. Work on building your connections and becoming more attuned to your emotions to heal the limbic system. By the time you create positive habits in those areas, then you will be ready for healing the cortex in chapter nine. Many other factors play in to the healing of our brains and bodies, some of which we have control over and others we have no control over. Just as you had no control over experiencing ACEs, you had no control over your genetics or family of origin, both of which determine so much about your body and how it functions. However, they do not necessarily determine who you will be. This is up to you.

Along with the research on neuroplasticity, scientists have concluded that you have multiple genes passed down from your parents that may or may not be expressed at your time of birth. These are often called genetic predispositions. As you go through stressful events, the negative genetic predispositions can become expressed. Imagine toggle switches on your genes that can be flipped. For example, when I was completing my Master's degree (which was a very stressful time in my life due to overwhelming amounts of responsibility at work, family, home, and school) a genetic predisposition for gluten-intolerance switched on. Interestingly, research has shown that you can also switch the genetic toggle switches back the other way. Again, this is such hopeful news!

At this point in my life, I have noticed that gluten is less of an issue than it used to be, but that darn sugar is still a trigger. Of course, the question that lingers in your mind may be: how do we flip the toggle switches? The journey may stretch on for years, but as you practice being Lucky with the tools in this book, things will change. You will begin feeling a peace beyond understanding, gratitude that fills your soul, relationships that heal all past wounds, and the ability to control being present in the moment without the nagging thoughts about the past or fearful thoughts about the future.

Take a moment and sit with this right now. You may look at your life and doubt the possibility of such a statement. Or, you may accept the overpowering hopefulness fueling your excitement on toward a Lucky future filled with healing and significance. You are in control of your thoughts and choices. Choose wisely.

Hello, Patience.

Sensing Calm in Your World

Another area where genetic predispositions and family of origin meet (possibly creating waves of hopelessness due to your lack of control) include sensory issues. Here is another way to recognize that your body falls short of perfection, and the importance of placing your value in your True Self. As previously mentioned, the primitive brain handles the primary senses. Most people know the five main senses of touching, tasting, hearing, seeing, and smelling, however, three other very influential senses play a role in the way you perceive the world. First, your *vestibular* sense contributes to balance and orientation in space. It is the leading system informing your brain about your movement and the position of your head relative to gravity. Second, your *proprioceptive* sense helps you understand the position, location, orientation, and movement of your body muscles and joints. Proprioception provides you with the sense of the relative position of neighboring parts of the body, and the effort used to move body parts. Third, your *interoceptive* sense relates to your internal sensations of the state of your body including hunger, thirst, heart rate, respiration, and elimination.

Regardless of how fascinating our senses are, why is this important to understand? First, it helps you build empathy for yourself and others. Sensory deprivation and sensory overload exist, but most people do not recognize them as such. For example, when you see someone wanting to spin, twirl, ride the merry-go-round, ride a motorcycle, or just need to feel the air against their body, then the vestibular senses need stimulation. Their body and brain are telling them that they need to meet this need for their brain to calm down. When people are persistently running in to things, jumping into things, hitting or tapping stuff with their body, they are meeting their proprioceptive needs. Examples of sensory overload include people who can't handle strong smells or loud noises. Imagine having an itch and being told not to scratch it. Do you abstain or do you scratch it? You scratch it, of course! Your body is screaming about a fundamental need to be met, and for you to respond.

People who experience sensory issues have much less control over their response to sensory overstimulation or deprivation than most believe, especially children. More control is gained with age, but this is not always the case. An occupational therapist can assist with these needs, perhaps by practicing a variety of exercises. As you read about sensory issues, you may have had some lightbulb moments for yourself or about others in your world. Recognizing that people often lack awareness about sensory issues and have little control over them, has this newfound knowledge increased your empathy? What does that feel like in your body right now? Where do you feel it? Just witness, without judgment.

In addition to building empathy, understanding your senses can also guide you in ways to calm your body. For example, you may notice that you gravitate toward auditory input. Meaning, when you are stressed out, you can choose to listen to relaxing music as a way to simmer down. Or, you may notice that vestibular input soothes you. Therefore, you can elect to go for a bike ride when you are emotionally dysregulated. Use this information to your benefit as a means of calming your limbic brain, giving you greater access to your cognitive brain. This is just another way to take control over your brain and allow for neurogenesis.

Taking Control over Your Body

The following will be a brief overview of areas you have control over that impact your body, genetic predispositions, neurotransmitters, hormones, etc. that were gifted to you through your genetics and family of origin. The information is not intended to shame or guilt. I ask you to read the facts, witness the thoughts, emotions, and body sensations that surface. Do your best not to judge yourself based on this information, and if you feel compelled, please make a note of ways you can learn from this to build a future plan for success.

Sleep

Research (and possibly your own personal experience) has shown that a lack of sleep or restless sleep can manifest as symptoms that get diagnosed as mental illnesses including depression, anxiety, and Attention Deficient Hyperactivity

Disorder (ADHD). Do you really have control over the quality of your sleep? Yes, more than you may think. Briefly, you can give yourself the permission to sleep, manifest bedtime rituals, create a comfortable environment by decreasing light and noise pollution, keep work out of your bedroom, eat a complex carbohydrate before bed to increase serotonin production, avoid clock-watching, and practice relaxation, mindfulness, and meditation techniques.

It is also essential to understand how caffeine and other stimulants affect your body. Caffeine can stay in your system for up to forty-eight hours, decreasing the quantity and quality of your sleep. You must first recognize your sensitivity to caffeine. I am not suggesting that you wake up tomorrow and avoid all coffee, tea, soda, and other forms of caffeine to test out this hypothesis for yourself. If you do not consume hefty amounts of caffeine, then you could try a more extreme approach. However, if you drink copious amounts of caffeine daily, then you need a month-long, gradual decrease before avoidance can be a part of your strategy. This paragraph may make it seem as though you can quickly fix poor sleeping quality. Each of the steps above takes time, effort, planning, and practice, but, quality sleep is possible. Give yourself permission to hope, especially if you have given up in this area, or if poor-quality sleep has had a negative impact on your functioning.

Diet

Food consists of more than the sum of the nutrients. You can take capsules or drink all of the necessary nutrients needed for functioning and still be less healthy than those eating whatever they want. Think of food and eating as an experience that incorporates culture, emotion, and relationship. Each time you eat, all of these factors play an active role in your food choices, and the effect food has on you.

My food choices used to be very rigid as an attempt to heal my gut, which made the experience stressful and unappealing. I love food! However, the stress I had preparing meals became more of a cost to my body than the benefit of choosing the "right" food for my body. I did not realize at the time that being so stressed out about my way of eating was actually taking me further from my health goals.

Eating such a strict diet even affected my relationships. My wife and I would avoid going places because the "right" foods were not available. Remember our conversation about how relationships heal the brain? We were unknowingly keeping our bodies from the generous curative properties of connection.

Are there benefits to following stringent diets? There can be, and for some people it is crucial. For example, individuals with diabetes must limit their sugar intake. However, if you do not have any serious chronic diseases and find yourself constantly feeling guilty or shaming yourself for eating or not eating a specific way, then you may find yourself in a similar place as I was, where the stress of eating caused more damage than the health benefits.

Having been in the alternative medicine and health food industries for many years, I am going to offer my personal conclusion about diet. Balance, in every sense of the word, is the best medicine. Meaning: balancing eating healthy with allowing yourself treats, all in the midst of grace. If preparing food causes an extreme amount of stress on a particular day, then you will be better off eating conveniently and stress-free. Never avoid relationships because of food. The connections in your life are of much more value. I understand that my genetic predisposition of gluten-intolerance can be a real eating limitation. I also recognized that as I began to let go of the stress of eating, my body became less affected by eating gluten when it was entirely inconvenient to eat gluten-free. Food for thought.

For those looking for a general guideline for eating healthfully, I like Michael Pollan's formula from his book *The Omnivore's Dilemma*: *Eat real food, not too much, mostly plants.* Eating *real food* means shopping fresh. Spend more time on the outside perimeter of the grocery store where you will find fresh produce, fresh meat, fresh dairy, etc. The main idea is to consume mainly the food you can raise or grow. You can't grow or raise a corn chip, therefore, limit your intake of such products. Eating *not too much* means consuming regular meals and snacks, every three to four hours, in a relaxed, comfortable setting (as best you can). If you were using a Likert scale to assess your level of hunger (where zero is starving, and ten is brutally stuffed), attempt to stay between a three and a seven. Eating *mostly plants* can be visualized by filling half of your plate with produce at a meal. As always, listen to your body. You are the expert of your body, and you know better than anyone else what you are feeling, what foods make you feel terrible or energized, and how your diet affects your stress level. Diet and emotion are as important to assess when eating as the nutritional content. Keep it balanced.

Over the past couple of decades, with the help of brain

imaging technology, research has been accumulating on what is now being called the gut-brain axis. The gut-brain axis can be thought of as two telephones. One phone in the brain and the other in the gut connected by the spinal cord and vagus nerve (which links our emotions and cognitive functions in the nervous system with our digestive functioning). Imagine that you are really worried about a big event happening in your life. How do your emotions effect your gut? You may notice a lack of appetite, nausea, loose stool, constipation, or even just butterflies in your stomach. It is all connected.

Another clear example of the interplay between the brain/nervous system and your gut is in depression. I do not want to get too technical, but the nervous system has chemicals called neurotransmitters. When they are in balance, they allow you to feel normal. When the neurotransmitters become imbalanced, they affect your emotions and physiology. Research has shown, serotonin, norepinephrine, and dopamine imbalances correlate with depression. Most people do not realize that up to ninety-five percent of the body's serotonin is found in the gut. Your gut greatly influences your mood and cognitive abilities, while your mood and cognitive abilities significantly affect your gut. Working toward a healthy gut by eating balanced will help you think more clearly, concentrate better, and feel better emotionally and physiologically.

A final word of caution: when everything in life feels out of control, your diet can be one natural area to become hyper-focused on in an attempt to gain control. You are learning many tools in this book to put into your tool box of control. Food does affect you, but you have several other ways to gain power over your life, other than your diet.

Become aware of balancing all of your areas of control. Please seek out professional help if this is an area of concern.

Movement

This is everyone's favorite subject! You likely know, research has shown that movement and exercise reduce stress, balance neurotransmitters, increase self-esteem, enhance cognitive performance, help control addiction, have the tendency to improve the quality of sleep, have the tendency to increase energy, enhance neurogenesis, and decrease the effects of trauma. Phew! Most of this information probably comes as no surprise.

In my experience, one of the most important aspects of movement is finding what you enjoy to do in your body. To plan for success, you will likely have to take pleasure in movement, or your routine will not be consistent. To benefit from movement, you need to get your heart rate up to the point of being out of breath for approximately twenty minutes. Walking is my favorite form of movement because I can do it daily with other people, which builds connection as well. If I only have five minutes, I shake and dance. Put on your favorite song and cut loose!

I am not going to belabor this topic because we all know we need to move. You may be really triggered by the subject of movement. Witness it. Create awareness around it. Then you can decide what you want to do with it.

Breathing

Hello, Patience.

No really. The next aspect you have control over is breathing. It is something you do every day, but you may not be reaping the benefits if you are not spending a few minutes with Patience. As we discussed in the first chapter, practicing soft belly breathing (focusing on the in-breath and out-breath for three to four counts each, for up to twenty minutes a day) can result in many physical, mental, emotional, relational, and spiritual benefits. I'm hoping that you and Patience have become good friends through this journey, and will continue your relationship far into the future.

Laughter

This may seem like an odd topic to address, but it is an essential aspect of health. Intentionally including laughter in your life can offer a wide array of benefits. For example, Norman Cousins had a sudden onset of an autoimmune disease called collagen disease, which was very painful. He stated, "I made the joyous discovery that ten minutes of genuine belly laughter had an anesthetic effect and would give me at least two hours of pain-free sleep." What was he doing? He was taking responsibility for what he had control over. He had no control over the disease in his body, but he was able to take away the pain for two hours at a time. And he did.

One day I was sitting with a colleague in my office chatting about a busy day. The topic of laughter came up, and we began discussing the health benefits of incorporating laughter into our client's lives, as well as our own. I remember saying, "I know the benefits of laughter, but I always tend to choose horror movies." We looked at each other for a moment and then laughed for the next ten minutes. It was probably the first time that horror movies had brought about laughter in my life. Since this moment, I have been attempting to incorporate more entertainment that gives me a good laugh.

Time in Nature

When was the last time you had an experience with nature? Perhaps you just spent time in the grass, at the beach, by the woods, in a park, by a lake or river, or in some other way connected with nature. What does it do to your body? How does it affect your spirit? If you cannot remember the last time, then put it on your calendar right now. Spend ten minutes sitting with your eyes closed becoming aware of the ground beneath you, the smell in the air, the feeling of sun and/or wind on your face and body, the sounds around you, the feeling within your body, the energy deep within. Do you feel a sense of gratitude as you connect with nature? A sense of awe? Note that time in nature is different than participating in activities in nature, which would be categorized as a movement. You may realize the difference in benefits as you try sitting in nature, as opposed to being active.

Research has shown the benefits of spending time in nature to include better short-term memory, restored mental energy, stress reduction, reduced inflammation, better vision, improved concentration, sharper thinking and creativity, possible anti-cancer effects, immune system boost, and reduced risk of early death. These are the benefits to the body. I am going to leave it to you to witness the benefits to your spirit.

Connectedness

I am aware that we just spent an entire chapter on connectedness, but since we are identifying ways you have control over affecting your body healthily, let us acknowledge the importance of how connection affects your physiology. If you did not realize it before this book, you will now fully understand that humans are relational beings. Dr. John Cacioppo from the University of Chicago has conducted numerous research studies and written countless journal articles on the effects of connectedness and loneliness. He concluded that isolated creatures die sooner, "from humans to flatworms and fruit flies." Several other researchers have concluded similarly.

Coronary heart disease is currently the number one cause of death in the United States for men and women. Several studies have shown a direct correlation between benefits in cardiovascular functioning and experiencing positive social support. Whereas social isolation has been identified as a heart health risk. Health psychologist, Kelly McGonigal, brought one aspect of the health benefits of social connectedness into popular media through a TedTalk. She described how the stress hormone (oxytocin) releases when two people hug, which heals the damages of stress.

A neurologist from Stanford University, Robert Sapolsky, has been working with baboons for over thirty years and has come to several interesting conclusions through his research. What does research on baboons have to do with you?

To understand Sapolsky's research, you need to appreciate how stress affects your body. The body's stress response was intended to keep people safe by increasing adrenaline and energy to either fight or flee. However, humans are experiencing the stress response as a direct result of fearful thinking without any immediate threat. Unfortunately, in this situation, your body cannot keep up with the production of the neurotransmitters and hormones that give you the adrenaline boost while balancing the other chemicals in the body that can cause damage to your system in high amounts. Yes, cortisol. Over time, you begin to experience one or more of the following results of long-term stress: increased heart rate, high blood pressure, reproductive system vulnerabilities, brain chemical imbalances, compromised immune system, higher risk of heart disease (due to the increased plaque in the arteries directly caused from stress), brain cell death, decreased memory capabilities due to hippocampal degeneration, increased dangerous fats in your midsection, switched on genetic vulnerabilities and predispositions, and a shortened life. Ultimately, chronic stress increases the risk of heart disease and other chronic illnesses while creating an inadequate environment for promoting happiness and productivity.

For years, Sapolsky watched how alpha dominate male baboons created a living hell for the subordinate baboons, which caused the subordinate baboons the exact same adverse health problems and vulnerabilities shown in humans who experience chronic stress. However, in one of the communities, the baboons ate tainted meat from a nearby dumpster and ended up with tuberculosis, which killed off many of the male baboons. After grieving for the baboons, Sapolsky realized one clear predictor of the baboons who survived. The baboons who were socially connected survived.

The gender balance shifted to twice as many females as males. With the alpha male baboons gone, it left only "good-guy" males who treated each other and the females with a certain amount of respect. Over time, the baboon's bodies where showing the positive health consequences of living in a lower-stress environment. They exhibited normalized blood pressure, heart rate, stress, and immune system markers, etc. The most exciting aspect is that after twenty years this particular baboon community continues to experience the benefits of this change. Large-scale lasting change is possible! If baboons can do it, we can do it!

More remarkable research between connectedness and your physiology includes mirror neuron. Mirror neurons are nerve cells in your brain that respond when you perform a specific action, and they respond in the same way when you see someone else perform the same action. For example, the first time you got your heart broken was probably excruciating, and such memories are not quickly forgotten. When you see someone else experience a similar breakup, the mirror neurons in your brain respond and allow you to tap into the same pain you had as if you were re-experiencing it. Some people call this sympathetic resonance, others call it neural Wi-Fi. What this means is that you are hardwired to resonate with others. Mirror neurons give you the capacity to understand others. They allow you the ability to tap into another person's emotions and energy. Have you ever talked to someone and felt like your energy was completely drained from your body? Again, you can thank mirror neurons.

Just like regular Wi-Fi, you can turn your neural Wi-Fi on and off at will. In the last chapter, I discussed how sympathy or sympathetic resonance can pull you down into someone else's pit. This is true, and it can take you to a place you do not want to go. Similarly, it can allow you to experience other's positive emotions, as well. Do you know someone who gets excited about something, and when they share it with you their excitement and energy transfers into your body somehow? Again, thank mirror neurons. You are hardwired for relationship. You need others, and they need you. Your relationships with others act as a heuristic tool that can teach them how to be healthy and heal. Likewise, you can become healthier, as well as heal when you are surrounded by those who resonate health.

This may bring up a genuine quandary in your life. Are the people you are surrounding yourself with propelling you toward health and healing or dragging you down into a pit? You do have control over turning on and off your neural Wi-Fi, but the more time you spend with people in a pit, you may not even notice that you have allowed your neural Wi-Fi and sympathetic resonance system to stay online. The cynical and pessimistic messages find their way into your body, mind, and spirit and degrade your own positivity.

Caroline Leaf, a cognitive neuroscientist, has shared images of neurons that are healthy and thriving and those that are affected by pessimism and negativity. They look staggeringly different. The healthy neurons resemble a beautiful forest, whereas the neurons affected by cynicism and negativity look like thorny bushes. You do not live in a vacuum. People affect you, and you, in turn, affect other people. Throughout this journey, I hope that you find the tools to be a change agent in your world who becomes excited about life and positively affects others down to their neurons or even deeper. This will add to your Luckiness.

Hello, Patience.

Lastly, researchers have been highlighting inflammation as the root of multiple chronic diseases including heart disease, diabetes, cancer, and Alzheimer's. The inflammation response is the body's way of trying to ramp up the immune system to either heal wounds or fight infection. However, just like the stress response, too much of a good thing creates chronic inflammation and leads to an increased risk of disease. What diseases or illnesses tend to run in your family? Can you assess any patterns in your family that may have contributed to these familial issues? What can you learn from these patterns?

To increase hope and control over factors that contribute to chronic inflammation you can take responsibility for your diet, exercise, environmental toxin intake, chronic stress, hostility, household dysfunction, neglect, and isolation. It is probably no surprise that diet and exercise decrease inflammation. Environmental toxins may seem like a factor you have no control over. However, you surround yourself with environmental toxins if you use body perfumes, artificial scents to help your house smell good (i.e., Glade plug-ins), artificial scents in your car, and other synthetic products you put on your skin. Essential oils are an excellent alternative for allowing your body, house, car, and office to smell fresh without the negative health results.

As for decreasing stress and hostility, you have learned many tools in this book, including spending time with Patience, movement, and connection (to name a few). You will continue to learn more, all the way until the last chapter. Increasing healthy communication in your home along with focusing on your True Self are two key ingredients that will change the atmosphere in your home if you are experiencing a dysfunctional (or even a relatively functional) home life. Lastly, understand that connection acts as an anti-inflammatory and decreases your risk of chronic disease. I hope that you begin to enhance your experience with healthy, optimistic, dream big, level five, interdependent, True-Self-focused relationships, for your body's sake. Also, your Luckiness depends on it!

As we close the chapter on your biology, be aware that help is only a phone call away. Many qualified and caring individuals are scattered around the globe waiting to help you take control over your body. You are not alone. Further, your body is significant because it houses your True Self, regardless of the onslaught of media advertising that glorifies the False Self through the body. Remember that your body is still only a shell; you are not defined by your body. However, you need your body, and it would do you well to care for your body as you maintain anything else important in your life.

All the chapters in this book gradually build upon the previous ones, therefore, place this chapter appropriately in the order of importance for which it has been written. The fact that everyone sees your body can compromise your perspective on its importance. Do your best in the moment. Learn continuously to recreate your success plan often. Be aware when you are taking yourself too seriously. Remember to celebrate life!

The Gift of Luck Stages of Change

Healing brain and body through sleep, diet, movement, breathing, laughter, time in nature, and connectedness.
Communicating empathy, assertiveness, and collaboration.
Connectedness through interdependence.
Fearless Purpose. Truth, Trusting, Faith, and Risk.
True Self Identity. Self-Love and Self-Acceptance.
Hope. Control. Self-responsibility. Priorities.

8

Why do I do that?

I want to celebrate you coming this far through the journey! You have overcome so much at this point in the process, as you have worked through all the exercises and stopped to practice deep breathing. I can only imagine how different you must be feeling! I envision you climbing a mountain and looking back at all the beauty you experienced behind you as you eagerly await the completion of your adventure.

What has benefited you the most thus far? What aspect of the journey sticks out in your memory? What has been your greatest challenge? What areas do you find your greatest strengths? What areas do you want to prioritize to be intentional about growing? As you reflect on these questions and your journey to this point, your introspection leads us precisely to the topic of this chapter. Awareness.

I love my oldest son so much. This is important to state before I share with you an area we have been working on together for years. Since he was a child, he has struggled with sensing his surroundings. In the past, he focused so much on what he was doing and what was in front of him that little effort went into seeing, hearing, or sensing anything around him. To his credit, most teenagers exhibit the same behavior. My wife and I repeatedly attempted year after year to encourage increased self-awareness. When he ate, he seemed to chew four times, swallow, and finish his plate before the rest of the family took more than a few bites. I used to say that there was no way he could taste his food.

After he received his driver's permit, he finally began to understand the importance of awareness. I sat in the passenger's seat explaining that he had to take in the whole scene in front of him at once to know what was going on around him to get him safely to where he wanted to go. He said that he couldn't do it. We talked about how as his awareness develops he will learn to notice brake lights three cars ahead of him before the vehicle directly in front of him even begins to brake. He will see the light changing to red even when he sits tenth in line. He will become aware of cyclists coming up on the right, where his car is positioned in the road, and everything else going on *all at once* to keep him and others on the road safe. His pattern was to direct his attention on the car bumper directly in front of him, worrying too much about the guy behind him, and daydreaming. He is, as we all are, a work in progress, but he finally understood the importance of awareness. In truth, I was the same way! My wife and I have worked hard toward my growth in this area, as well.

Up to this point, I have asked you to begin creating awareness in many areas of your life including hope, control, responsibility, identity, value, love, acceptance, significance, fear, faith, trust, risk, connectedness, communication, biology, genetics, neurology, and physiology. In the last chapter, we discussed the eight senses (sight, smell, sound, taste, touch, vestibular, proprioceptive, and interoceptive). Without this knowledge, you would find difficulty in other chapters, but even more so in this chapter.

Simply put, Luckiness does not happen without self-awareness. Understanding where you are, where you have come from, and where you want to go to intentionally grow takes a significant amount of honesty and self-reflection. This began in chapter one and will continue through our journey's end.

Self-awareness is another way to gain more control and hope. As you become cognizant of what helps you and what limits you, then you can work toward change. When you learn from your past and use that information to plan for a better future, you gain control, and hope rises. By now, you know that without hope and control, your motivation to change will be next to nothing. Without motivation to change, you will never be Lucky.

Body Awareness

Throughout this book, you have mainly been creating a self-awareness of your interior world. Self-awareness of your interior includes the sense of interoception, emotional intelligence, understanding your values and belief system, personal strategies within your roles, energy, and spirit. As a refresher, interoception allows you to witness and understand physical sensations within your body including respiration, heart rate, pain, tightness, hunger, fullness or satiety, energy, the urge to urinate or defecate, tingling, itching, or burning inside. Many times throughout this book

I have asked you to witness what you are experiencing in your body, which has begun to strengthen your awareness of interoception.

Why is it so important to be attuned with what you feel in your body? Your internal bodily sensations act as a warning system about what is coming or what is already happening. Understanding what your body is telling you allows you to catch problems in your life before they become overwhelmingly big.

Think of your body as a vehicle. This is not far off because your body is the vehicle for the True Self. In your car, when a low oil light illuminates your dashboard, you know that it is time to do something to make the light go away. You may decide to add oil, change the oil, replace the seal on the oil pan, or whatever allows you to solve the problem. The body continuously gives you cues, just like car alerts. You would be wise to treat your body better than your car because you only get one of them, and at this point, you cannot trade it in for a new one. Just as a car requires maintenance, your body needs to be maintained to allow you to live out your life's mission and vision. The only way you can catch problems before they become very costly or unfixable (like your car) is by becoming attuned to your body.

Like most, I have found that my stomach tightens when I get stressed out. However, as I become aware of my body's warning system, I have options. I can continue allowing stress to accumulate in my body, which leads to many other problems in life (as previously mentioned in the last chapter). Or, I can spend some time with Patience, go for a walk, listen to calming music, or one of many other relaxation practices. What is the benefit? My mind concentrates better and thinks more clearly. I feel more connected to my True Self. I can be the best version of myself in my relationships, and they can flourish as opposed to suffering from the emotional reactivity that accompanies being stress out. Further, if I de-stress at the first warning, then my body will not need to give more cues, such as increasing inflammation, forming additional plaque in my arteries, producing more unhealthy fat in my gut, or any of the other natural negative consequences of not being attuned to your body.

Tuning In

How do I become attuned? What am I trying to feel or find? To become attuned to your body, you begin by stopping. (Yes, you read that right). Stop whatever you are doing, even if for just a moment. The first couple times you practice listening to your body, it may feel strange or uncomfortable. One way to practice is by completing a quick body scan. Start in your head. What do you notice? Any physical pain, tightness, pressure, heaviness, or other sensations? Can you feel the pulse in your temples? Continue to move down your body witnessing, not judging, tension in your jaw, clenching your teeth, stiffness or tightness in your neck and shoulders. Notice any heaviness in your chest, fullness, hunger, burning or tightness in your stomach, or other sensations in your midsection. Sense any aching in your hips, pain or tightness in your knees and ankles, warmth or coolness in your hands, feet, or any other sensation in the rest of your body. Sometimes the words to describe the feelings can be difficult, which creates even more awkwardness. This is a typical experience and absolutely okay.

Now that you have assessed what is going on in your body, you have the choice to either do something about it or allow it to continue. Sometimes you will act and other times you will not. Each time it may look different. When I feel the tightness in my stomach, I may only have sixty seconds before I have another client, or I may have an hour for lunch. What I do will depend on the amount of time I have. Other times, I may notice it and do nothing. No judgment. However, to plan for success, you can practice spending time with Patience often, especially in those times when you only have five to ten seconds.

Hello, Patience.

What about pain? Does pain medicine mask the body's communication and create more problems? When you notice that you have a headache, for example, your body is attempting to communicate that something has gone awry in your physical system. Pain can be challenging to assess, and headaches can top the list of frustrating pains. If you have a headache it could be from dehydration, a lack of sleep, a sensitivity to the environmental chemicals around you, the effects of eating or drinking something your body is reacting to, an imbalance in hormones or other internal chemicals, the adverse effects of stress, or a laundry list of possibly more severe problems. As I said before, depending on time and resources your actions may look different at any given moment. If the headaches are frequent, then seeing a doctor you trust would be a good idea. If the headaches are infrequent, then try to identify on your own what has caused them because this allows you to practice how to learn from your body and past. This also gives you the option of planning for a more successful future.

When I get a headache, which is infrequent, I tend to drink a glass or two of water, take a nap, breathe deeply in the cleanest air I have available, stretch, and assess what I recently consumed. Other than rest, my assessment does not take very long. If I don't have time for a nap, I may opt for an Ibuprofen to support me until I have time to nap. As you listen to your "check engine lights" in your body, you become more attuned with your body. Keeping up your bodily maintenance allows you to catch other problems before they become unmanageable, in addition to allowing you to continue striving toward your life purpose. You know how difficult it can be aiming to be the best version of yourself when your body feels chronically miserable.

Emotional Intelligence

Next on the list of creating a self-awareness of your interior is emotional intelligence. The Center for Creative Leadership reports that emotional incompetence accounts for seventy-five percent of career failures. That is a staggering statistic! Aristotle stated, "Anyone can be angry--that is easy. But to be angry with the right person, to the right degree, at the right time, for the right purpose, and in the right way-- that is not easy." Emotional intelligence starts with understanding your own emotions, but it reaches deep into the lives of those around you, which has a generational effect.

What does it mean to understand your emotions? Begin by recognizing that you feel various emotions every moment of every day. Emotions fluctuate momentarily. Consider a morning your favorite daily breakfast food was not available. You may feel irritated and hurt that your spouse didn't consider your needs when they forgot to pick up the one food you wanted, as they were grocery shopping. You might feel stressed with work-related problems, and you needed a good breakfast to get you going. You may feel hopeless that the day is starting out so poorly. To your surprise, your spouse tells you that your favorite breakfast food was put away in the wrong place. In one moment, all of your feelings change. It is important to note that everyone else's emotions do the same thing. Emotions continuously fluctuate. We can trust this. Understanding this is another step toward empathy, which could also be labeled other-awareness.

Happiness and other positive emotions including excitement, joy, gratitude, serenity, interest, hope, pride, amusement, inspiration, awe, and love are typically the emotions people strive to feel and desire to portray. Often, happiness acts as the default emotion when no other strong negative emotions surface, such as fear, doubt, anger, guilt, sadness, disgust, impatience, hate, loneliness, jealousy, and insecurity. What does authentically happy feel like in your body? How do you know you are feeling happy? Sit with this for a moment. Tap into the emotion of happiness. Describe it. Perhaps you feel a lightness in your whole body without tension, peace within, and a slight energy in your chest that could quickly turn to excitement if allowed. You may find it hard not to smile.

As you sat with the emotion of happiness, you also may have become aware of the amount of control you have over your emotions. You might have found it easy to attune to happiness even if you were not necessarily feeling all that happy before doing it. What did you do? You changed your affect. Nothing outside of you changed. Not your situation, your relationships, your past, or your finances. You took responsibility for your emotions and deliberately altered them. This was not just a false portrayal of happiness that you pasted on your face to trick the world. You genuinely felt it. This practice is precisely what is meant when I say that you have control over your emotions. The more you practice bringing up positive emotions on demand when you are calm, the easier it will be for you to change your emotional state in times of dysregulation.

You may have had a hard time with this exercise. If you regularly experience depression, anxiety, or other mental health difficulties it may be severely challenging to just switch from one emotion to the next. But, it is possible. Do your best to allow that hope to spread within you. Accept it. Embrace it. Look forward to a day when you can. I have seen it. You can be the next success story.

Consider the intensity of your emotions. You may be feeling mildly happy, moderately nervous, moderately excited, and highly fearful in any given situation and moment. Identifying the severity of your emotion is a helpful exercise. Try communicating this the next time you share your feelings. Most people simple say, "I am angry." However, you may be frustrated, irritated, angry, furious, or enraged. Notice how the severity of the emotion appropriately increases as we communicate with different words? As you begin to understand the intensity of your emotions, you will unintentionally broaden your emotional vocabulary. This helps you connect with your body and accurately reflect to others. When you accurately reflect, they will feel wholly understood, heard, and loved.

The terms "positive emotions" and "negative emotions" may lead you to believe emotions can be good or bad. This is not true. Emotions are a natural bodily response to your internal and external environments. You have the privilege of experiencing all the negative emotions at every intensity. When you have not allowed yourself to experience intense negative emotions, then how are you going to honestly feel the intensity of positive emotions? Emotions are a gift we get to experience. They are what make life interesting. Life is uninteresting when you only pick and choose from a small handful of emotions for fear that you or those around you cannot handle your big emotions. The tools in this book can help with managing your big emotions, as well as others.

The most problematic aspect of experiencing emotion is controlling the behavioral expression of the emotion. However, I can be enraged and still not hurt myself, others, or property. Even as you sit here, you could potentially bring on the feeling of rage. The extremely heated energy reaching out to every part of your body, the fullness in your head that feels like you could explode. But that does not mean you have to yell at someone, hit the wall, or throw something. Instead, you have the option of going for a walk, talking it out with someone, writing it down, or many other possibilities. Allow the feeling of rage to subside by spending a moment with Patience.

Hello, Patience.

Even though it may feel uncomfortable at first, it benefits you to share your emotions honestly with others in your level four and level five groups. Boundaries may need to be set to let them know that you do not need advice or want to be *fixed* when you share that you are experiencing a negative emotion. Communicating your emotions allows you to connect with others in a more profound, authentic way. This offers both of you a more meaningful interaction, especially when the other person can relax knowing that you are not looking for them to change the emotion. You and I recognize the control you have over changing your emotions whenever you want. Remember, you are feeling more than just that one negative emotion at all times. It may seem counterintuitive to sit with a negative emotion instead of changing it to positive all the time, but you can learn so much about yourself, your belief system, and your motivations as you begin to spend time with the negative emotions. The hardest part is holding back judgment of the emotion, and instead merely seeking to understand it. You will find that once you discern why you are feeling a certain way, the emotion drastically decreases, as a result.

The last important aspect of creating emotional intelligence is in recognizing and accepting that emotions do not equal truth. Have you ever felt an emotion so strongly that it influenced you to believe something based on the feeling alone and no tangible evidence? For example, you just "know" that so-and-so did not say hello to you because they don't like you, even though you did not say hello to them. Or, you just "know" you are going to have a bad day today based on the feeling you had when you rolled out of bed. When you build reality on the way you feel, this is called emotional reasoning. Emotions alone do not offer adequate evidence to say something is the truth. Can feelings lead to truth? Yes. But, you should not trust your emotions without supporting proof because, as previously indicated, emotions constantly fluctuate, whereas what is true and real should not. Can you think of a time when you used emotional reasoning? What was the outcome? What can you learn from that experience?

What are You Thinking?

Continuing the exploration of awareness of your interior takes us to revisit your values and belief system. As previously mentioned, your belief system acts as an essential change agent within you because what you believe influences your emotions and your emotions influence your behaviors. If you are looking for a Lucky behavioral change shift, then your belief system is integral. Think about where your hope begins. Hope starts with a belief. You believe you have a certain amount of control in getting from point A to point B, which allows you to feel hopeful. When you believe someone is For You and With You then you feel secure. When you believe you are being heard, you feel loved.

How do your emotions and behaviors change because of these beliefs? If you feel hopeful, you are more likely to attempt to change. If you feel that you are loved, accepted, and safe then, you are more likely to make an effort to improve. Everything discussed in this book is a piece of the puzzle for change action and the more puzzle pieces you acquire, the more and more likely you are to create behavioral change and be Lucky. I hope your experience is congruent with this statement.

Now that you understand the importance of your belief system, how do you create more awareness around your beliefs? Ultimately, creating a habit of questioning your motivations will lead you to understand which beliefs have influenced specific behaviors. *Why did I do that?* This could be a helpful reflective question to gain more awareness and allow you to learn from your experiences.

The fact that I was young when I started my family gave me the opportunity to reflect on my belief system often. My motivation was to be a good father and a good husband. I did not always make choices that reflected growth, but the motivation was strong. My wife stayed home to raise our children, which we both believed was important. Even though it was a priority for both of us, there were times my wife would share, "I feel like all I am is a mom and nothing else." In those moments, early on, I really could not understand what she was feeling for many reasons. First, I believed that I was in charge of making her happy. As we both now know, I had no direct control over her happiness. Therefore, when she made statements like this, I took it as a personal offense that I was not good enough as a husband. I became defense, instead of empathetic. Second, I believed that her identity as a mother should give her ultimate purpose in life. Not only that, she got to stay home to do it. Problematic thinking abounded in my young self. My perspective stemmed from my experience of frequently being away from home due to work and school. All I wanted was to be home with the kids, which tainted my empathy. Next, any time you base your identity on what you do, you are strengthening the False Self, which I did with my wife. Not only that, I was *shoulding* on her; believing she *should* be happy because I was doing my best even though my best had nothing to do with her emotions regarding her identity. Lastly, who am I to understand God's purpose for her life? Her purpose is something I can support her in discerning for herself, but I could never know what she needs to feel fulfilled in her True Self. I know, daft right? Thank goodness we always have the opportunity to learn.

As you read through my story, do you see how questioning your motivation and creating awareness of your belief system can better your life and the lives of those around you? At this point, I am able to hear my wife without making her frustrations about me, and my empathy has increased exponentially. Instead of trying to *fix* her to *make* her happy, I reflect what she is thinking, feeling, and the meaning underlying her communication, which helps increase her internal awareness and personal motivation to change. Instead of attempting to steal her control (which comes across as trying to control or manipulate her), I empower her by letting go of what I thought was my responsibility for her emotions. This is a much different approach than I had for many years. As a result, it has instilled a belief within her that I am For Her and With Her even though I cannot make her happy or determine her path and purpose in life. These changes in my belief system obviously have changed my behaviors and have crafted a very different set of glasses through which my wife sees me since those early years. Most importantly, we have experienced a much happier and healthier marriage between us.

As you begin to understand the importance of your values and belief system, I hope that you become increasingly more intentional about looking at specific beliefs to assess whether they are healthy, based in truth, or helping you toward your goals. As you may have noticed, we have been diligently working on changing your belief system since our journey began together in chapter one, and will continue until the last word of this book. The most critical and impactful beliefs we have include beliefs involving value, control, responsibility, identity, purpose, and connectedness. As long as you have (or are working on) those particular beliefs, then you will find yourself in a much better and Luckier place. Of course, through your journey, you will find beliefs that are limiting, unhealthy, and just not accurate. Fear holds the gloves for being the ultimate contender in your battle for truth. The champion of the fight is up to you!

Relational Strategies, Part II

Continue your path to awareness by recognizing your behaviors as acted out through your personal strategies in your relationships and roles. Your strategies can significantly affect the extent to which you and others trust you, your attainment of personal autonomy, your ability to take responsibility and control, and your capacity to see your True Self. Let us look at a few examples of relationship and role strategies to offer a few mental pictures of what I mean.

As a manger, if you tend to give in to everyone's requests, what might your strategy be? You might be trying to gain approval from those working under you. The reasons for this can vary greatly, but one aspect of your strategy is clear: you believe saying "no" makes you mean, and you fear being mean. What is your truth assessment? Remember, assertiveness holds to the belief that everyone's needs are equal, which includes your own, the company's, and the employee's. Do the best you can to meet all three needs (which is not always possible), but you will gain more respect from the employee through the negotiation process, you will feel good about yourself, and the employee will likely stay longer in their position. Some might argue that a collaborative approach takes too much time, but when you create raving fans out of your employees, the positive energy and emotion transfers to the customers. Your employees are usually the first and last contact a customer has, which will also be the aspects of their experience they remember most. Remember, relationships are absolutely vital!

As a spouse, what happens if you find yourself holding back physically and emotionally from your spouse? What is your strategy? Fear again. You likely were wounded deeply in the past or even a current relationship. Trusting someone in that way once more seems difficult, if not impossible. You may be thinking, *I've got you, I wasn't wounded in a relationship*. Let us go back to attachment for a moment. Did your caregiver offer you physical or emotional support when you needed it? As we previously mentioned, of course, you learned this strategy. No blame. No shame. Just awareness. You get to decide what to do with this awareness. It would help to accept that the strategy of keeping everyone at arm's length falls into the category of unhealthy. Yes, I'm going to repeat it, we *need* relationships.

Let us look at one last example: how might a strategy in one of your roles be limiting? As a friend, you may give advice every time someone even hints that they are struggling with a problem. You may provide amazing and wise advice, but if someone does not ask for it, then they may begin distancing themselves more from you over time. What is your strategy? You may have a need to feel superior. Why? There could be different reasons, but you likely don't really believe that you have inherent value aside from your behaviors (False Self), and you have to prove your value through acting "smart." This strategy, among others, limits us in our relationships. The more aware of the relational strategies you are, the more likely you can overcome them with healthier strategies, and the result will be healthier, happier relationships and a Luckier you.

Listen Deeper

The last awareness of your interior that it is crucial for you to connect with, the deepest level, incorporates the energetic and spiritual level. What do I mean by this?

Let us look at what science can tell us. Science has shown us that you are composed of cells. If you keep zooming in you find that the organelles comprising your cells are made of molecules (for example, H_2O is water). If you zoom in to just one hydrogen atom, you find a single proton and an electron. The majority of us have been taught that protons and neutrons create a core where electrons furiously orbit around the core, held in orbit by an electromagnetic force. Like most other things in science, our knowledge has progressed. Were you taught that Pluto was a planet? Me, too. Just as Pluto was demoted, physics continues to discover more about the world around us. The new physics suggests that subatomic particles can be viewed not only as physical particles but as patterns of vibrations. Therefore, many scientists believe that at our lowest physical level, you and everything you see around you is composed of energy vibrating at different frequencies. Even Albert Einstein concluded, "Everything in life is vibration."

Earlier we discussed sympathetic resonance, where the

mirror neurons within you respond to the people with whom you interact. Understanding that you are composed of vibrational energy may help in understanding new physics as well as mirror neurons. In truth, I still kind of think of Pluto as a planet. Change is hard. Is it better to be right and believe a lie or change and understand the truth? The beauty of life is that you get to choose what to believe. Just remember, your belief choices dictate the consequences (positive or negative).

In addition to the deepest physical level, I have discussed my belief that you are also spirit. This is the essence of life. The body houses the soul, the True Self. How do we tap into both the energetic and spiritual aspects of ourselves?

Creating awareness at an energetic and spiritual level takes time and practice. Is it possible? I (along with many others) choose to believe that it is. How? Just as you become mindful of any other sense in your body by narrowing your focus to that particular sense, you can direct your full attention toward either the energy field or the spiritual realm. For example, when you want to really listen to something, what do you do? You close your eyes, shut your mouth, direct your awareness away from touch and smell, and lean into the sound with focused, intentional awareness. The same is equally true of the awareness of energy and the awareness of spirit.

I believe that as a human in the physical world, composed of vibrational energy, you have a form of connectedness. Just like physics, this is not yet fully understood by science or religion. However, it effects how you think, feel, and act. With a body composed of vibrational energy, it would make sense that just as your body has difficulties with illness, disease, or infection, your imperfect body can also have problems at an energetic level that need to be managed. Additionally, as a spiritual being, you have the potential to connect with our Creator. These are two separate parts of your being (energy and spirit), yet both directly and significantly influence everything about you.

Interesting food for thought, if you believe that God spoke humans into existence, then it would make sense that humans at their most basic physical level are frequency or vibrational energy. I believe that you have the potential to become attuned to the Creator and others around you through both of these parts of your being, which fulfills the highest potential of a human and a spirit. Attunement cannot be attained without awareness of these aspects of yourself.

Most people use either prayer and/or meditation to get to a state of mindful awareness of the spirit or vibrational energy. Personally, I use prayer, meditation, or something I call "prayerful meditation," which combines the former two. Begin by spending time with Patience in a comfortable position, either lying or sitting in a place free from distractions and that has a sense of safety. Close your eyes and feel yourself in the space by checking into all of your bodily senses individually. This helps to ground yourself in the moment while clearing your mind. Then begin focusing on your inhale and exhale while progressively relaxing from the top of your head to the bottom of your feet, releasing any and all tension. At this point, it becomes difficult to describe in words how to tap into the awareness of energy and the awareness of spirit, but here goes.

Begin with the awareness of energy, which we have discussed is vibrational in nature. Think of the vibration as that consistent, predictable, repetitive pattern we discussed in the last chapter that has an ebb and flow, just like your heart pumping blood through the veins and arteries in your body. In the past, in moments of relaxation and awareness, you may have connected with the feeling of your energy and decided (just like your neural Wi-Fi) to turn your awareness off because it felt weird or different. You may have little to no conversation about energy or spirit awareness in your life. Ultimately, you did not know what to do with the feeling and awareness, so the most reasonable choice was to turn it off.

The first time I really understood this feeling was during an Integrative-Based Stress Reduction (IBSR) workshop, which is a somatic therapeutic modality to release stress and trauma from the deepest parts of the body. Research has shown that your body holds on to your stress and trauma deep within your nervous system and muscles. When your brain is fixed on a negative belief or a traumatic event, at some point your thoughts become distracted and begin thinking about something else. The nervous system, however, continues to communicate the traumatic message and ruminates on it in the rest of the body, which can cause the adverse physiological problems we previously discussed. In the next chapter, we will discuss what else to do with the stored stress and trauma in greater detail, but utilizing attunement to your energetic level can help in releasing the trauma from those deepest parts of your being.

The energetic movement was most natural for me to notice in my arms and hands first, but you may feel it elsewhere, or all over your body and through your body. Have you ever laid your hands on someone to pray over them? You can feel the energy in your hands as your hands become warm. Even as you sit here reading, you may find that you can feel a tingling in your hands. Find someone you trust who is willing to help you because this may be an easy exercise to attempt to tap into the vibrational energy within. Hold your hands about an inch from their shoulders and become acutely aware of the feeling in and around your hands as you speak love, intention, and prayer over them. It will likely be an experience you will never forget.

Another example that may help in understanding the energy within and all around you includes times when you walk into a room where others have just been in a heated argument. The negative vibe or uncomfortableness in the air can be tangible. The individuals could have stopped many minutes before you entered the room, but the energy around the room can still be felt.

If you are still struggling with the idea of becoming aware of the energy, then you have a couple options. First, you may decide that the rest of this book has been helpful, but you are not resonating with this message. Therefore, you can skip over this and keep reading. Absolutely fair. Second, you may be intrigued, but need further help. Do your best to find someone in your immediate world to help you with this at the moment, or reach out to *The Gift of Luck* team.

Creating awareness of spirit can be the most natural or most challenging part of you to connect with. Just as with the energetic connection, your experience with the spiritual connection may be a little different than my own. When I practice prayerful meditation with my eyes closed, I create a space in my head behind my forehead where I invite a connection to God through the spirit. Often the space becomes brighter as the connection becomes stronger. Others have shared a similar experience. During prayerful mediation, I choose a scripture verse to meditate on. For example, 1 John 4:18 "There is no fear in love. But perfect love drives out fear." While dwelling on a verse, I continue to keep that space available for any additional messages from God.

In your attempt to connect with God in your inner space by inviting Him to communicate with you, please be careful of what you invite in. In college, I had a terrifying experience when I attempted to ask God in, and instead of the brightness I discussed, I felt a blackness that I allowed to come in, and I quickly regretted it. You have the power and discernment to keep yourself safe from evil as you invite the divine to take root in your life.

I have attended Catholic, Baptist, African, and other non-denominational spiritual events where people talk about feeling the spirit move. As you progress in your awareness of each, you will begin to better discern between the two. You will get there, just continue practicing, connecting, and witnessing your experiences within. Again, if you are not connecting with the messages of awareness of energy and spirit, then consider your options of what you want to take from them, and what you want to discard. If nothing else, I hope that you take away the need for silence and solitude through meditation, which is a universal practice that benefits all.

I heard a story of a workaholic businessman who was seeking self-actualization. He was told of a guru who could help him attain his goal. When the man finally met the guru, he explained his goal of self-actualization. The guru said that the man would need to start practicing meditation for fifteen minutes a day. The businessman tried to negotiate a different approach. He emphatically expressed to the guru that he did not have time to meditate fifteen minutes a day and that there had to be some other way to be self-actualized. After thinking for a moment, the guru said, "I think you are right that you do not need fifteen minutes of meditation a day to become self-actualized." The businessman felt relieved and excited to find out a substitutionary approach. Then the guru said, "You need one hour."

Feeling like the businessman? If you are seeking greater growth, joy, fulfillment, attunement, and Luckiness in your life, then you cannot overlook the necessity of silence, solitude, and introspection leading to awareness. Martin Luther King, Jr. indicated that the longer and more difficult he expected the day to be, the more time he would spend in prayer in the morning, even if that meant getting up earlier. The benefit of silence and solitude must have overpowered even the value of extra sleep. Now that we have completed the discussion of self-awareness of your interior, the next step is creating a self-awareness of your exterior. A break with Patience seems appropriate.

Hello, Patience.

Other Awareness

Once you have an awareness within, creating awareness of everything around you is a much smoother process. Why is this important? If you are reading this book, I would assume you want to help yourself heal, learn, and grow. I hope that you also have the intention of assisting others to move toward positive change as well. Indeed, this is the design of *The Gift of Luck*. You learn it, and then you pass it on to someone else to heal, learn, and grow. If you are not aware of the world around you, then you will have no influence over it. If you notice that people draw close to you to talk about their personal struggles, then you understand the opportunities created through the open invitation of Being With them. If you have not experienced such a connection, then creating more awareness of the exterior may be an area in which you want to grow. You get to decide.

Going from being a therapist serving adults to working with children in play therapy and other child-friendly therapeutic modalities, I had to learn the language of children's behavior. I had to gain an understanding of when they needed to explore, when they needed a welcome home, when they needed their emotions organized, when they needed boundaries, and when they needed me to verbalize how I was For Them and With Them. It is only natural that these skills lead to creating more awareness, not just for children, but for adults as well. After all, we are just big kids trying to figure this all out. You are not alone in that.

Noticing and being attuned to others' thoughts, emotions, and behaviors while seeking to understand that person in the moment can be described as empathy. Empathy is the basis for self-awareness of the exterior. Empathy affords you the opportunity to look into the lives of those around you and understand the strategies they have learned and are practicing. You may be able to recognize the strategies without empathy, but empathy allows you to see the learned strategies more clearly and without judgement. Empathy can help others heal and begin the path to teaching strategies that are helpful and not limiting.

Think back to our discussion about relationship strategies in chapter five, which included interdependent,

dependent, independent, and disorganized strategies. If you remember, the healthiest strategy in relationships is interdependence. However, when we attempt to narrow all of our interactions into four categories, it makes it extremely difficult, doesn't it? Think of the four strategies as simple guides to understanding the belief system behind the general strategy. For example, sometimes I am tired and not really willing to engage with others the way I would if physical, mental, or emotional fatigue were not in play. Other times, I may have a headache, and I just cannot focus. Just because every relational interaction does not exemplify interdependence at its best, it does not mean that I do not believe in and strive for interdependence. I am not going to do it perfectly, and neither are you. And that's okay.

To complicate matters, not only do we imperfectly practice interdependence, you may have noticed that your own personal strategies change with different people in different settings. Your strategy with your spouse may be different than your best friend, the people at work, the people at church, or strangers. Of course, the same is true for everyone else. No wonder relationships can be intensely challenging at times. Begin with empathy, and you can't go wrong. Recognize that other people's strategies shape their capacity for relational intimacy, how close they cling, how they keep you at a distance, their ability to heal from past relationships, or their ability to grow through struggles in their relationship with you. Remember, you, I, and others create strategies to allow us to feel loved, accepted, or safe. Can you blame us all for trying?

Self-awareness of the exterior is mainly an awareness of others, but it is also aware of your surroundings in general.

There is a world that exists outside of you. You are not the world, only a part of the world. Be a healthy contributor to the world.

Realizing that the towel you just hung up dropped to the floor, and picking it up communicates to your spouse that you value the way they keep the house clean. Recognizing that a piece of trash fell out of the trashcan, and picking it up. Noticing that another person is out of coffee as you are refilling your cup and asking them if they want theirs topped off. These seem like minute details in life, but being aware of your exterior, and taking responsibility for such actions communicates volumes to those you care about. Further, in these little details of life, you are crafting the glasses through which they see you. In the beginning, in the end, and all the way through life, it is still about relationships. You cannot force others to treat you in this way, but you can be the person you want others to be as you model it.

Careful What You Choose

This is the perfect segue into understanding self-awareness of choice, which is the final area of emotional intelligence. The concept is easy to comprehend. Every decision and choice you make for yourself has a ripple effect. Often we do not want to admit that our choices affect us, others, our future, and the future of others. Indeed, one devastatingly poor decision has the potential to alter many of your family generations to come. That is a pretty heavy statement that could quickly be paralyzing. No need to let the fear of doing everything right and perfect keep you from living life. Life is meant for mistakes, learning, and growing.

As we create an awareness of our own personal choices and how they influence us and others, it can help us to make decisions that benefit the future for all of us.

Your choices influence and, in many ways, create your internal environment with a feedback loop. You make decisions that either support or go against how you already think of yourself, which can either make you feel good about yourself or create an internal dissonance. You are not your behaviors and actions, but your behaviors and actions influence how you and others see you, just like glasses you craft for others through your nonverbal communication. Do your best to focus on identifying with your True Self, but recognize that when your behaviors do not align with your True Self, then you tend to feel the negative emotions associated with identifying with your False Self. The more you work with the tools in this book, your choices and behaviors will support your True Self, enhancing the positive impact you will have in this world. As a result, the behavior feedback loop will reinforce the True Self, which allows you to feel authentic, confident, and Lucky.

For example, the decision to take on an additional project at work may influence you in multiple ways. If you take on the project, then you may feel more valuable at work, yet more stressed because you have less time. This may affect your physiology in numerous ways, including stomachaches, headaches, and sleeplessness. In turn, your choice may strain your external environment in the relationship with your spouse, children, family, and friends. Further, your choice could affect your future and the future of those around you at work, at home, and in the community with the way you spend your time. I am in no way implying that a decision is right or wrong, because such choices remain between you, your spouse, and God, but be aware that your choice does affect you internally, externally, futuristically, and generationally. This awareness can allow you to invest in the aspects of life that you want to prioritize. Have you checked on your backpack of stones lately?

Is any recent decision or choice coming up for you right now? Maybe it even happened this morning. How has the choice affected your internal environment, and how you view yourself? How has it influenced the external environment and the significant relationships in your world? In what ways do you foresee (as best you can) the ripple effect into your future and even the fates of those who depend on you? Would you make the same choice again? How would you change this choice if a similar situation demands a future decision?

As you look around at the other people in your life, notice how people show their life priorities through their choices. If your father spent most of his time outside of work watching television, drinking, playing golf, serving in the church, or spending time getting to know you, then whatever he chose to do reflected his priorities. Many people work really hard to get ahead financially or positionally, which provides a particular type of secure environment for their spouse and children. This is absolutely honorable. However, these choices are best when they reflect a balance between work and relationship. If you are providing well for your family at the expense of not spending time with them, then you may want to reconsider what your choices communicate.

Full disclosure. I strive to prioritize my life as follows: God first, my spouse second, my children next, and then everything else. When I think about what my choices reflect to those around me, I do not always like what I find. I have to be acutely aware of my decisions around overworking at home to communicate to my family that no competition exists between my priority slots for them and work. To mitigate such a message, I wake up before everyone else for my own quiet, reflective, and future-invested work time. After a day at the office it would be easy and natural for me to spend my evening working on personal projects, and at times I do. However, intentionally choosing through awareness which projects, how often, whether I can include my family, and so on, helps me to be more attuned to what I am communicating through my choices. I don't always make wise decisions, but my awareness of choice grows increasingly over time. What do you notice is surfacing for you right now? What priorities are reflected in your decisions?

Choices reflect priorities, and they also communicate purpose. If you are a teacher, then you will find your choices reflecting your own purpose of conveying wisdom and knowledge to others inside and outside of work. If you discover purpose in healing, then your choices may show how you strive to learn and offer more effective methods of healing throughout time. If you find purpose in helping others, then it would make sense that your choices, time, and behaviors are spent serving. This will look different from person to person, but the overall choices speak clearly as to a person's purpose.

What would it look like if you began making choices differently, motivated by the purpose of working with others as a part of something bigger than yourself connecting you with people and the divine, instead of making choices driven by Fear? Close your eyes and sit with this for a moment. What would this look like in your life? What daily decisions do you make that are motivated by Fear? Maybe you are noticing that it is not the daily choices that need to be changed. Perhaps you need to make a decision to refocus your life purpose from an isolated self-focused motivation that has not offered the fulfillment you expected. Maybe you want to become connected. Perhaps you want to join in on the purpose of helping the greater good. Isn't self-awareness fun?

Only you can look within and be honest with yourself to assess if your skills match up with your purpose and dreams. Perhaps you have aspirations, but your training lacks what is required. Personally, I would have loved to begin helping people with mental health issues without education and training, but looking back, I now know I could have done more harm than good. Regardless, do not allow this step to deter you. Decide now that if you have a particular calling and life purpose, then it is worth your time and finances to be able to fulfill that purpose. More than that, you will be used for more good, and more people will be changed for good as a result of your investment. Find your sweet spot where you can feel fully utilized while doing something you love. Any idea what that looks like?

The ultimate goal of becoming self-aware of choice is to create a better life for yourself, the lives of those around you, and the world as we know it. It all starts with you! It starts with your choices. Do your best to invest in your future self!

In this chapter, have you noticed that without self-awareness not a single aspect of this book or growth in your life can be accomplished? All your time spent with Patience, assessing your mind, body, and spirit does not exist without self-awareness of the interior, just as evaluating connection fails without awareness of the exterior. Awareness of choice affects all areas of mind-body-spirit-connection. Therefore, even though we have discussed all the vehicles of change in chapters one through seven, the key to the ignition of your vehicle is self-awareness. No need to lock the keys in the car and walk away. Let's go for a spin!

Self-awareness of your interior, exterior, and choice.
Healing brain and body through sleep, diet, movement, breathing, laughter, time in nature, and connectedness.
Communicating empathy, assertiveness, and collaboration.
Connectedness through interdependence.
Fearless Purpose. Truth, Trusting, Faith, and Risk.
True Self Identity. Self-Love and Self-Acceptance.
Hope. Control. Self-responsibility. Priorities.

9

Becoming whole

Do you know the feeling of excitement, joy, energy, and connectedness accompanying moments in your journey when you are able to accomplish a goal related to helping another person? As a therapist, I feel extraordinarily blessed by the daily opportunity to join alongside others in moments when they experience a new success. Those powerful "ah ha" moments are what make my job worth it. It is exciting to think that you are gaining the skills and enhancing your ability to create an environment of change where these moments may be experienced increasingly in your own life.

Do these moments usually happen when you feel physically ill? Do these moments typically occur when you are mentally exhausted? Emotionally spent? Frustrated in your relationships? It can, but it is exceedingly more difficult.

When I come home after a ten-hour day of practicing therapy with children whose lives are troubled, and where trauma is their norm, my emotions and reactions are directly connected to how well I take care of myself. My wife and children get to see me at my best and my worst. The most significant factor in whether they receive a husband or father who is present and meeting their needs stems from that day's practice of self-care. My motivations can be pure, my intentions can be attuned to the needs of my family, but if I am not taking care of myself, then they suffer.

Bringing Life, Not Pain

Your self-suffering magnifies others' suffering. Your self-suffering can inhibit those you serve from more growth. Self-care is not just important, it is vital to being who you want to be, vital to the successful application of playing out your purpose, vital to the relationships in your life that you care for so deeply. The word *vital* connotes a sense of keeping something alive. Things die without their vital signs. Your self-care is vital to you, to others, and to your future.

As a general guideline, *self-care* is understanding and practicing stress reduction, directing anger in a healthy way, processing sadness, working through grief, and coping with any other situation and emotion keeping you from being the best version of you.

Changing the culture of your lifestyle to care for yourself begins with permission. Give yourself permission to take time to respond to your own needs. As a result, you will be capable of being fully present and healthy for those for whom you love. What does this bring up for you? Sit with this for a moment if you are noticing a reaction. Bring awareness to this moment, and witness the emotions and thoughts surfacing. Your self-awareness affords you the opportunity to decide if you want to make a change or not. Likely if you struggle with feeling burdened, overworked, and overstressed, then you may not want to address self-care, but you also know that you are the most in need of self-care. Take this time. You and others will benefit immensely.

Hello, Patience.

The Great Balancing Act

Our view of the quantity of time can supersede quality of time in our relationships. As a parent, I have felt guilty for even thinking about taking that precious time away from my family to practice self-care. Can quality time be genuinely shared with your family when you are filled to the brim with anxiety, frustration, sadness, grief, or the like? Be honest with yourself and everyone else, no one is superman or superwoman. No one can hold it all together and participate in quality relationship building without self-care.

When you have a family, the balance is delicate, yet critical. If your job causes so much stress that your time necessary for adequate self-care prevents you from meeting the needs and responsibilities of your family, then it may be time to rethink some aspects of your life. Do the rocks stored in your backpack need to stay in your backpack? Do you need to rethink your career choices? What are you communicating and modeling to your family about the priorities of a healthy life? What do you want the balance to look like in your life? These are tough questions but essential to ask when life feels off kilter.

Finding the balance of how you practice self-care could look significantly different (or even opposite) than the way your best friend handles self-care. I have shared that I walk, practice deep breathing, shake and dance, practice mindfulness, practice prayerful meditation, and have a glass of wine a few days a week (don't think I mentioned this last one). I have found this works for me most of the time. Other times I need more. Sometimes self-care looks like holding hands with my wife, playing with my kids, or having an engaging conversation with good friends. The ultimate goal is decreasing stress, feeling centered and grounded, and having a sense of your own personal cup being filled.

One misconception of self-care that must be addressed: self-care works best when you are stressed out. False! Liken your stress level to that of a balloon. When you become stressed, you add air to the balloon. Each occurrence you take for decreasing your stress level, air is able to deflate the balloon. When your balloon fills too much, or your stress level becomes too great, you explode. Before the explosion, it only takes something minute to burst your bubble. If you are able to keep your balloon half full or less, then you will be able to think more clearly, handle the daily problems that accompany life, and be the person you want to be, instead of being a reactive, miserable, guilt-ridden shell of a person.

Self-care incorporates much of what we have already discussed, which is helpful because you have already begun your transformative journey. Similar to how Mr. Miyagi taught Daniel Larusso the art of karate in the movie Karate Kid (by sanding the floor, painting the fence, washing and waxing the cars), throughout all of the chapters in this book you have been learning many forms of self-care. First, you have been spending time with Patience multiple times in each chapter, which has been teaching you how to include deep breathing in your day. Next, you have learned elements of mindfulness, including being present in the moment, seeing the past as your teacher, and learning from the past to use what you have learned to plan for a more successful future. Third, as you communicate assertively within an interdependent relationship strategy, your stress level will decrease. Also, during the discussion of what you have control over in your biology and genetics, you learned that sleep, diet, movement, laughter, time in nature, connectedness, and your sensory needs can work as focal points for self-care. Lastly, silence, solitude, and introspection through prayer, meditation, and attunement have been discussed as forms of self-care, as well. Let us look at a few other options.

More Self-Care Tools

Guided Imagery

Guided imagery acts as another great form of relaxation and self-care. At the beginning of the first chapter, you experienced a progressive relaxation guided imagery. Many versions of guided imagery can be found on the internet. Some of the ones that I use more frequently include creating a "safe place." Your imagined safe place could be the beach, a garden, your grandma's living room, Mars, or even heaven.

Another version of guided imagery is called the Wise Guide. The wise guide has many versions, but it may take you to a place in the woods where you see a figure walking toward you, who is your wise guide. You ask the wise guide representing your True Self or the Spirit of Truth to give you wisdom about any question you have. As with all guided imageries, the goal is to bring in all of the senses to make the experience as real as possible. In many ways, it is not much different than hypnosis.

As we stated early on, your brain has trouble differentiating between reality, imagination, and dreaming. For this reason, hypnosis or even placebo can be effective tools. If you are dealing with chronic pain, for example, multiple hypnotic methods exist that successfully decrease pain incuding chronic back pain to daily headaches. The key aspect that plays into the effectiveness of hypnosis is the hypnotizability of the individual, and the amount of self-hypnosis practice. Research indicates that approximately two-thirds of the population is hypnotizable, of which five to ten percent are highly hypnotizable. Why is this important? I want you to understand the tools you have available for self-care.

Creative Expression

This can be an exceptional self-care tool, which takes many basic forms including art, drama, dance, music, or writing. The type of creative expression you tend to gravitate toward will dictate the supplies you need to keep on hand. Writing and journaling are the primary ways therapists urge clients to begin practicing creative expression because the supplies are readily available. Whether using pen and paper, a purchased journal, a computer document, a journaling app, a vocal recording, or any other way to get your thoughts, emotions, ideas, and dreams recorded in some way, this allows you to get everything out without the fear of forgetting something. This also allows you to stop thinking about it. Often I suggest rereading your journal entry one to two days after writing with the goal of identifying mistruths and rewriting truth. Other forms of art, including drawing, pastels, painting, ceramics, woodworking, etc. benefit a person in similar ways by allowing one to emote and have a physical representation of thoughts, feelings, or dreams as to not forget them.

Music

Creating a playlist of music for different moods can also be beneficial, and allows you to plan for success. We often listen to music that reflects the mood we are experiencing, as opposed to listening to music that helps our bodies relax. For example, when you feel angry your music choice may be heavy, loud, and fast. This can act as a form of empathy because it reflects how you feel, just as a friend who listens, understands, and reflects back to you helping to organize your emotions. This music choice may be helpful for a song or two, but if you continue to listen to the heavy, loud, and fast music, your body will tend to stay amped up. However, if you listen to calm music, after a song or two your body tends to mimic the mood of the song. Remember, your body (at its most basic level) is frequency. Therefore, it makes sense that your body tends to respond to the frequencies and moods of music. You have the choice to use music to your benefit or your detriment.

Dancing

Have you ever experienced a night-long dance, whether in high school or later in life? The movement and physiological benefits of dance as it releases stress and trauma from the body can hardly be matched. One unique difference exists between dance and other forms of exercise like walking, running, or working out. Dance gets your body moving, but also offers space for emoting through creative expression, which may mimic what you are experiencing in your life. During the dances of your youth, it may have been very awkward, not because the dance was awkward, but because your fear of looking foolish held you back. If you surpassed the fear of judgement and cut loose on the dance floor, then you expressed what you were feeling: free! In college, I began swing dancing. It was one of the best releases of emotional energy and expression I have experienced in my life. I still receive the benefits, because every time I think about those dances, I always smile.

Performing Arts

The art of drama, acting, spoken word, poetry, and the like can have a positive impact on your stress level. These areas served for years as expression and emoting in my life. You gain the benefit of relationship in drama and acting, which offers exponential benefits (as we have discovered). Further, sharing your creative expression with others through all of these avenues unlocks fear, provides an opportunity for receiving empathy and can lead to connection with others. I challenge you to try one of these creative expressions within the next two weeks. Note how you feel before, witness the feelings during the entire process, notice what happens afterwards regarding fear, value, love, acceptance, safety, and connection, and write everything down to help you mindfully learn from the experience.

Hello, Patience.

Emotional Charge for Change

One particular emotion sticks out above the rest regarding creating a life worth living and can be a form of self-care. Excitement. Close your eyes right now and conjure up the physical feeling of excitement. If you find it difficult to bring on the emotion, think about a time when you experienced something exciting, and then tune into what you felt at that moment. Feel the energy bursting forth from your chest and head, the warmth that heats your back, increases your heart rate, forces you to smile, and influences you to get up out of your chair because of the overwhelming hopefulness and gratefulness jettisoning you into the next second, minute, hour, day, week, etc. Are you with me? Imagine a life where you experience this feeling daily, every night when you go to sleep and each day as you awake. Do you think you would ever get tired of feeling it? I know I don't. Is it possible? Maybe not every day, but more days than not. Would that be different than how it is for you right now?

How can you make steps toward a life where this is your reality? Dreaming. Not in the sense of sleeping. Dreaming about a future where you live out a life you deem the "ultimate fulfillment." What would that look like? Notice if the answer comes easily or difficultly. If you can easily rattle off what your dream would look like, then you are already on your way to spending time daily or at least multiple times a week to conjure up the excitement of pursuing such a future.

If you are on the other end of the spectrum, you may

feel confused and frustrated because you have no idea what to dream about, or maybe even how to dream. In these circumstances, consider exploring with a dream partner. I have multiple dream partners in my life. First and foremost, my wife and I spend many conversations talking about what we want our future to look like, after considering what we learned from our lives so far. Creating time and space to dream with her evokes the emotion of excitement, hopefulness, and gratefulness, in addition to drawing us closer together and deeper into an emotional connection in our marriage, even during times when we share fewer overlapping interests or time.

Can you see how dreaming about the future (alone or with others) acts as a form of self-care? Dreaming really takes us back to chapter one as we covered the topic of hope. The excitement you experience when dreaming about the future can be considered the zenith of hope and acts as a great form of ridding yourself and others of hopelessness.

The importance of self-care has been detailed along with a host of options for action, but it needs to be personal for you to commit this stone to your bag of priorities. Which option or options called out to you? What benefits do you expect? What will it take to incorporate self-care into your life? Plan for success for yourself to be the best version of yourself, which will lead to the ability to positively influence those around you and be Lucky.

Hello, Patience.

The Gift of Luck Stages of Change

Self-care through deep breathing, mindfulness, connection, guided imagery, art, drama, music, dance, and dreaming.
Self-awareness of your interior, exterior, and choice.
Healing brain and body through sleep, diet, movement, breathing, laughter, time in nature, and connectedness.
Communicating empathy, assertiveness, and collaboration.
Connectedness through interdependence.
Fear versus Faith/Trust. Purpose.
Identity. True Self. Love, Acceptance, and Trust/Safety.
Hope. Control. Self-responsibility. Priorities.

10

Minding life

Throughout this book, an emphasis has been placed on your thoughts and belief system as they influence your emotions and, ultimately, your behaviors. Chapter five identified that your thoughts and personal beliefs are created through connection, which is a crucial player in healing, behavioral change, and being Lucky. In chapter seven, we further added to the discussion with two quotes from historical figures inferring that *you are what you think*. As promised, this chapter will dig deeper into how your belief system influences behavior and change, while addressing distorted thinking and mindsets.

To engage your mind, let us start with a couple of philosophical questions:

What is wisdom? Does wisdom exist?

What is truth? Is truth relative to each person or does ultimate Truth (with a capital T) exist?

What is a lie?

Controversy abounds on the answers to these questions, but what do you believe? It does not matter whether your answers are right or wrong. However, the fact stands that your answers influence your life, and the lives of those around you.

Believing Lies

Like most people, you probably hate when someone lies to you. Intentional lying must be one of my least favorite behaviors. Sometimes you accidently say something that is not true, but it comes from a place of misinformation. Other times, you believe something to be true, yet it is actually a lie or (maybe more accurately) it is rooted in a lie. This third infraction will be our main focus at this time.

What do I mean by believing something that is rooted in a lie? For example, if you believe you are a bad person, then you are using your False Self as the root of the lie that you believe. As we previously discussed in great detail, you are inherently valuable regardless of poor behaviors. This is the True Self. Believing the five word lie that *I am a bad person* can wreak such a storm of havoc in and through someone's emotions and behaviors. Let us play out this lie.

Here is a story of a teenage boy whose father lives in prison, and whose mother does the best she can to care for him and his three siblings. Due to mom's own upbringing and subsequent experiences, she reacts to her son's big behaviors by shaming him, which communicates that *you are a bad person because you do bad things*. The boy feels as though he cannot "do good" or "be valuable" because his identity is wrapped up in *I am a bad person*. Hopelessness consumes him as he knows he could not possibly have perfectly good behaviors, which seems like the standard by which he is being measured. Therefore, he accepts his fate as a terrible person. The young man's actions reflect his depression as he seeks out drugs and sex to give him momentary relief from his pain.

Further, he aligns himself with others who understand him, others who believe and feel similarly. From the outside, people have negative stereotypes of gangs. He calls his gang family. The effects are compounded with a brain riddled with chemical imbalances and a tattered immune system due to his ACEs (adverse childhood experiences), as well as an underdeveloped cortex due to his young age. The downward spiral continues with seemingly no hope of getting out, as he experiences trauma daily.

Does this seem so far-fetched? I see similar scenarios all the time.

If you have shamed your child in the past, does this doom your child to such a life? Of course not! We all have parenting moments for which we feel less than proud. When a child consistently receives the message *I am a bad person because my value is based on my imperfect behaviors* combined with other factors, it creates the perfect storm like this scenario. The child still has free will, but the perfect storm can be overwhelmingly difficult to weather, especially without a supportive connection. Do not forget that relational repair can happen, but it takes time for trust and True Self perspective to be built.

Another real danger in believing lies is the powerful potential toward suicide. Suicidal people believe *no one cares* and *the world is better off without me*. Both are lies. It may seem far-fetched to think that you could ever get to such a place. I hope that in the perfect storm, your beliefs and subsequent emotions and behaviors would hold firm. However, unless you, I, and others have someone communicating a different message, then life may be lost. Dramatic, I know, but this is the reality for our youth. And youth grow into adults. You see these adults every day at work, in stores, in your neighborhood, at church, etc. Perhaps, you are that adult. Hope is not lost. You are gaining the tools to create a new path for yourself and those within your circle of influence.

Hello, Patience.

By now, you understand the gravity of the beliefs you have about yourself and your world, and how they play out in your life. Other powerful harmful emotion-altering lies include:

I have to be perfect
I am not good enough
I have to please everyone
I am permanently damaged
I should have...
I cannot trust anyone
I am not lovable
I am not accepted
I am not safe

Many other beliefs profoundly influence your emotions, behaviors, relationships, and choices, but working on these will give you plenty to reflect upon for now. What if you find yourself believing one or more of these lies about yourself? What do you do? This may seem heavy and overwhelming, but I promise you will thank yourself in the end when you feel the rocks of Fear drop to the ground, lightening your backpack. You have multiple options to change your belief system. Being persistent to find what works for you is key.

Consider journaling about each lie to begin creating

awareness around the underlying memories or experiences that have reinforced your belief in each of these lies. Unfortunately, once a lie settles into your belief system, you look for reasons to confirm it (as opposed to disproving it). Therefore, you may find much to journal about. Throughout the process, practice some form of activity to help further process the emotions out of your body, i.e., walking, running, biking, swimming, shaking, dancing, yoga, etc. Consider setting your journal aside for a day or two before coming back to it, then read through the story of each belief and cross out the lies and rewrite the truth. Think about using a note card to write the belief at the top and the truths underneath. You can read it multiple times a day to change the belief. Do your best to become aware of when those beliefs are triggered during your day and speak the truth to yourself in those moments along with some form of self-care.

Imagine that your belief is like a path in a field created by driving a vehicle on the path over and over and over. You are attempting to create another track in a different direction in that field by driving over and over and over it, which forms a new belief based on truth. Changing the belief without any outside help takes practice and time. It is easy to forget that nothing worthwhile in life comes without a lot of work. Over time you will notice instead of looking for the lie in your experiences, you will subconsciously reinforce the truths, and then you will know you have changed! This can and will be your reality through your deliberate practice.

Other options include using your artistic abilities to create the new pathway of truth. You can draw, paint, collage, write a poem, write a song, or do anything else that allows you to express the lie and then rewrite your belief with an expression of truth. Consider bringing the truth into your daily prayer and meditation. Create an accountability partner and remind each other of the truth. Work with a counselor who can practice Eye Movement Desensitization Reprocessing (EMDR) or hypnosis. In my experience, EMDR or hypnosis can expedite the healing process. Regardless, like most everything in life: your results are directly correlated to your investment. Find what works best for you, create your plan, and begin. You've got this!

It is a perfect time to spend a moment with Patience.

Hello, Patience

Believing Truth

It has become abundantly clear how beliefs contribute to being healthy. How do they lead to being Lucky? In short, if you believe that you are inherently valuable, lovable, acceptable, and safe, then you are in a healthy space to work on tweaking your mindsets, cognitive distortions, and behaviors toward Lucky. Let us go back to our original questions of wisdom and truth.

Your definition of wisdom, truth, and Truth profoundly influence your mindset. If you believe that Truth exists and you seek it out, then you will learn, grow, and progress as a person because you are willing to listen to what other people have to say, without judgment, to test your own beliefs and change them if it gets you closer to Truth and wisdom. If you believe that Truth exists, but you either do not seek it out or are not willing to listen and learn from others, then you will likely miss out on the depth and richness of life offered through your personal relationships found on your treasure map of life. If you believe that truth is relative, and Truth does not exist, then you may spend more of your time defending what you believe as truth rather than seeking to learn from those around you. This will leave you stuck, stagnant, and possibly battling symptoms of depression.

I think we can agree that some Truth exists in the sense that life happens a certain way, regardless of our perception of it. For example, if I went to the grocery store and bought an apple, we can accept that as Truth because the actions I took happened a certain way. Even if you thought I bought a pear or went to a different grocery store (a personal perception of truth), it doesn't change the reality of what I bought or where I went. Therefore, some facts and Truth can be known regardless of a person's relative truth.

I'll never forget a debate my brother and I had over this, as we were driving in my 2007 Mitsubishi Outlander. I shared that I believed that Truth exists and the fun part of life is seeking it out. One major area of tension within the discussion was my interest in understanding how the world was created. He argued that I could never know for sure and the search was futile. We agreed to disagree, but we could both accept that regardless of what either of us believed happened, the creation of the world actually happened in only one way.

Choosing Your Mindset

The truth versus Truth debate leads us to the overview of our first of many mindsets.

Growth versus Fixed mindset

If you seek out Truth and wisdom, then I can assure you that your mind is primed for growth as you strive to learn and progress. Research is continuously reflecting on how your life will be more worthwhile and unbelievably happier when you adopt a growth mindset. Incidentally, a growth mindset is one aspect of mindfulness. As you learn from your past and others, you take that new information to plan for a more successful future. This is the most critical cognitive aspect of being Lucky! Seeking out ways to learn through self-reflection, talking to others, scripture, formal education, or other forms of learning challenge your current ways of thinking. This changes your behaviors and positively affects the way you view your own significance.

I love the church because it provides a weekly time for planned and intentional growth. However, books, magazines, TedTalks, podcasts, YouTube educational videos, and other opportunities to learn exist in abundance online and through phone apps. What form of learning do you find supports your growth the most? Which application is the most convenient? Which will you actually follow through on?

Opportunity versus Victim

During chapter six when discussing communication, I introduced the belief that all conflict is an opportunity for growth in a relationship between two individuals working toward collaboration because collaboration leads to increased emotional connection. If we continue to be a victim of Fear by avoiding conflict and collaboration then we do not grow, we remain stuck, we feel hopeless, and we find it easy to blame others for our own misery.

In the same way, you have the choice to look at life through the lens of opportunity or view yourself as the victim, as if God selected you as the receiver of all bad things. Let us speak the truth: bad things happen every day to everyone, just as good things happen every day to everyone. Most likely, you woke up today, you have a roof over your head, you have food to eat, and water to drink. You may even have a car, a job, people who love you, and good health. Were these already true today? All you had to do was wake up today? Sounds like a gift! So, without doing anything, you experienced multiple positives in your day. You are already starting your day with many beans on the positive side of the scale for the day. It almost seems unfair to the negatives because they are going to have a hard time catching up. What other blessings do you already start your day with?

Even bad situations can be opportunities in disguise. Several years ago, my family's health food store and clinic caught on fire. At 4:30am when the fire began, I struggled to see many positives, but as the days went on, I realized that the insurance money would allow us to rebuild in a way that would be even more advantageous to a prosperous future for the businesses. Think about some of the deepest pains in your life that you overcame including relationship loss, job loss, pride loss, etc. In moments of being an overcomer, especially of such terrible pains, I wonder if you concurrently experienced some of the most empowering, growth-filled moments of your existence. They made you, you!

As cliché as it is, every obstacle indeed is an opportunity if you decide to perceive it as such. It is your choice. You have the control. You do not have to be the victim of life circumstances any longer. Take responsibility for your life, embrace the hope that accompanies the newfound control you are perceiving, and be empowered to learn from the past to make a happier, Luckier life.

For some of you, this may all seem calloused. I do not know the struggles that you have experienced and continue to suffer outside of your control. You are right. However, focusing on all the things you have no control over draws you in to the victim mindset and will debilitate you. The antidote is to concentrate on what you have control over and taking responsibility for those things: your thoughts, your emotions, your behaviors, and your half of all relationships. If this is daunting, please reach out for professional help from a counselor or coach. Just do not let yourself stay in this pit any longer. Life is within reach, and you can still be Lucky!

Helping versus Limiting

This lens allows you to use mindful awareness to assess thoughts, beliefs, mindsets, emotions, relationships, strategies, stones, or any other aspect of your life. Throughout your day, you get to assess each moment by deciding whether you see it as helpful (which champions you toward your life goals) or limiting (which keeps you from your goals or slows you down). If you recognize that a cup of coffee in the morning gives you acid reflux, making your whole morning more difficult, then you have the choice to choose another beverage for breakfast due to coffee's limiting effect. If you notice that getting up ten minutes earlier to practice prayerful meditation influences a more positive attitude throughout the day, then you can choose to set your alarm for ten minutes sooner and/or go to sleep ten minutes earlier.

How about relationships? Who in your life influences you negatively or holds you back? Such a relationship may look like someone who negatively influences your perceptions or beliefs about yourself and the world. Or maybe they affect your emotions whether through stress, anger, sadness, or another negative emotion. Perhaps someone in your life influences your behaviors by directing you away from who you really want to be or what you want to do in life. Consider those who negatively impact the other relationships in your life. These are the types of relationship strategies you want to create awareness around, and possibly choose to set some boundaries. If boundaries do not work. Do you want to spend time with people who limit you or spur you on to greatness? You get to decide, but the latter leads to being Lucky.

Early on in my marriage, my wife and I attempted to set boundaries with a potentially important person in our life and, more so, our children's lives. However, he continued to cross the boundaries without remorse. The ultimate consequence included that we (unfortunately) were forced to cut him out of our lives. If boundaries do not work, the only choice is to build a wall, which is still a choice on the table. What other ways do you see using a helping versus limiting lens as beneficial for your life?

Investment versus Instant

Consistent with the three previous mindsets, this can be used as a lens through which to view many decisions throughout your day. Each choice can be considered to be an investment in your future, whether that be an investment in your future self, your family's future, your business' future, etc. The other option is to base decisions on what gratifies you right now. Other authors have used different words to describe similar ideas. For example, other professionals have labeled such mindsets as "rich" versus "poor" thinking or "long-term" versus "short-term" thinking. Each recognizes the importance of planning for a successful future by forgoing immediate indulgence.

Several years back, I went to an Investools workshop where I hoped to learn the necessary ingredients to becoming a prosperous online stock trader. I did not want to make investing a full-time job, but I had desired to increase financial stability while still pursuing my purpose in life. Even though my gift was not trading, I gained some valuable wisdom through the process. First, the trend of the market always rises over time, which means that if you purchase stocks with the intention of keeping them for a long time you usually make money. Second, all portfolios need to be diversified. Buying multiple long-term stocks will decrease the odds of losing large amounts of money. Third, get-rich-quick schemes do not exist. Everything takes hard work, time, sacrifice, energy, and resources. I attempted day trading, which means that I bought and sold throughout the day to make more money, more quickly, which focuses on the short-term rather than the long-term. After I lost three hundred dollars, I decided that unless I could dedicate all of my time to the art of day trading and relinquish my pursuit of my purpose, then day trading was not worth my time. Do any of these lessons apply to your life? Have you had similar experiences?

All this being said, it is essential to enjoy life in the

present, too. You cannot put all your happiness in the future because that day will never come. Focusing on balance in your life will yield higher returns by planning and budgeting ways to enjoy life now while planning for and investing in a prosperous future. Therefore, investment versus instant does not mean that you should only focus on the present, or only on the future. Or that one is good, and the other is bad. Find a balance that works for you and your future. What does that look like in *your* life?

Before moving into the next five mindsets, notice how the first four mindsets can be used as lenses through which to view life. Each of the last five pairs of mindsets can be considered to be on a continuum or a spectrum where the mindsets constitute the extreme ends, and you will find yourself somewhere between the two. Another way to approach the last five mindsets would be to rate yourself on a scale from zero to ten for each of the words in the pair, to understand the side in need of more practice.

Optimist versus Pessimist mindset

Do you have anyone in your life who continuously brings up the negative aspects of life, dwell on the negative, and would admit to being a complete pessimist (similar to the Saturday Night Live character Debbie Downer)? Wha wha wha. Perhaps you identify yourself as being that person. Whether you know someone like this or whether you fit the bill, witness what comes up for you right now. Even thinking about it, does it bring you joy, excitement, hope, happiness, or other positive emotions? Or do you find frustration, anger, resentment, hopeless, or other negative emotions surfacing?

In my practice, I have spent countless sessions with individuals who identify themselves as pessimists or a pessimist *and* a realist. More often both. First of all, notice that I said that they are in counseling. Typically, they present feeling unhappy and depressed. What is at the root of negativity and realism? Right, little to no sense of hope. I know by now you recognize that without hope all other aspects of your journey through this book would seem less impactful, little to no change would have happened, and the motivation to change would look more daunting. This is true of everyone. If your hope still wanes at this moment, then perhaps rereading chapter one would be helpful.

It may be helpful to answer the question, how is pessimism serving you? It can be a protective barrier when you are feeling unsafe, but it is likely holding you back from being Lucky. Consider how you can draw on hope and find other ways to keep you feeling safe.

Responsibility versus Blame

Think back to chapter one, and you will find that responsibility versus blame stems from your understanding of control. As you recognize what you have control over, take responsibility for your areas of control. Focus your time, energy, and resources on what you have control over, and then the degree to which you blame others falls drastically. Can other people's choices impact your life? Unquestionably, yes! Can you change them? Nope. Are you learning how to influence them? I hope so! Does focusing your time, energy, and resources on blaming others in your life for your misfortune help you to invest in your future? Definitely not.

If you used the same amount of time, energy, and resources to invest in your future through enhancing your half of the relationship by practicing healthy communication, setting appropriate boundaries, practicing self-care, learning through education, dreaming, and leaning into your life purpose, then you will be a much happier, healthier, Luckier version of yourself.

One of my best friends went through a divorce several years back, due to his wife's infidelity. He did not choose for it to happen, the pain was immeasurable, and it immensely impacted his life and his children's lives. Fast-forward a few years, and I had the privilege of officiating his marriage to the same woman. A few years later they divorced again due to similar circumstances. Talking to him soon after they decided to divorce the second time, his mindset was very different than the first time. He knew he could only focus on and control his own thoughts, emotions, and actions. The experience was still terribly painful, but he rerouted that pain into positive behaviors instead of destructive ones. He talked about wanting the best for his soon-to-be ex-wife but recognized that he had to set some boundaries to make sure he did not get hurt by her again. His mindful awareness and focus on responsibility instead of blame allowed him to grieve in a way that enabled for emotional processing while he invested in himself. This gave him a more hopeful spirit. As previously mentioned, blaming others gives away control, decreases hope, and leads to death. Control and responsibility produce hope and bring vitality to life.

Don't get me wrong, you need to hold others accountable for their actions to encourage change in your family, community, country, and world. Few things in life are black and white, all or nothing. Even blame used to stand up for what is good and right should be focused more on the solutions you have control over changing. Blaming just to blame is a dead-end street. Complaining just to complain, without focusing on a solution does not produce change. Using breath to complain is wasted energy that could be used for investing in a better future. Imagine if every person on earth chose one goal to focus on, banded together with other like-minded individuals, had an interdependent relational strategy, and worked for a purpose greater than themselves. Wow, what an amazing world this would be! You and I can do our part to bring this about.

Trust versus Fear

We spent many pages together in chapter three discussing trusting in something greater than yourself to decrease Fear. Fear was identified as one of the most significant deterrents to you becoming the best version of yourself, reaching your highest potential, fulfilling your life's purpose, and being Lucky. Even though Fear appears as an enormous, terrifying monster, in truth Fear is just a hologram. Fear is an illusion. Fear is an empty grave. You have complete control over Fear. Fear only exists if you allow it to survive. You give Fear power, and you can also take its power away. It is that easy, right? No, it is not that easy, yet it is possible!

How do I take control over my Fear? Each of us has different levels of Fear and to say that we all need the same prescription would be naïve and incorrect. Let us look at what you *can* do. First, decide that you are ready for the fight, and you are not going to allow Fear to influence your decisions any longer. The second step is going to look very different depending on your experiences. On one end of the spectrum, you may choose to do something because Fear has held you back, and you are electing to live with some uncomfortable feelings to take more control over your life. On the other end of the spectrum, you may have suffered extreme trauma and frequently experience symptoms of Post-Traumatic Stress Disorder (PTSD). Your fear response lies much deeper in your mind and body. In this case, your second step would be getting help from a trauma professional who knows how to help you overcome the fear response while doing your best to practice the self-care options in the last chapter.

For several years I have worked with individuals (both children and adults) who have experienced severe trauma. EMDR and/or hypnosis coupled with teaching mind-body stress reduction skills, mindfulness, and CBT have been very successful. You may or may not have realized it, but as you experience *The Gift of Luck* book and workshop, you are undergoing each of these modalities except EMDR. If you start including consistent, predictable, and repetitive patterns in your life, then you will likely notice how your brain can concentrate more easily, panic frequency and duration decrease, and your body relaxes more easily. If you practice these patterns while practicing your change of belief notecards, then you may experience even better results.

What will be your next best step in firing Fear as the co-pilot in your life? Remember, you need to begin by making the decision to take control over your life. Be prepared to live with some uncomfortable feelings that come in waves. Research shows that the emotional waves usually only last about ninety seconds, therefore, continue your practice with

Patience through the ninety seconds and you will make it through.

Hello Patience

Next, begin including consistent, predictable, and repetitive patterns in your life, including walking, music, jumping, shaking, dancing, tapping, etc. Continue your moment-to-moment practice of mindfulness. Make it a priority to spend time each day freeing yourself of unhealthy, limiting, and false beliefs. Soon you will find Fear has less of an influence than it previously had, and you will feel more empowered and confident. At first, it may seem strange that other people want to be around you more, but you will get used to it. People are drawn to individuals who exude Fearlessness.

Does this mean I have to start doing crazy or dangerous things to show how Fearless I am? Not necessarily, but you will find yourself trying new things you probably would not have attempted previously. One of the biggest Fears to overcome is the Fear of people, which will free you from many of the False Self-defeating lies because you know the truth in how valuable you are, regardless of behavior or mistakes. Once you understand and align with your True Self and disconnect your identity from the False Self while focusing on learning from the past and planning for a more successful future, then you have overcome many of the most defeating lies that people desperately struggle against: *I have to be perfect, I am not good enough, I have to please everyone, I should have..., I cannot trust anyone, I am not lovable, or I am not accepted.* Once you do not Fear people, then you may talk to people you never would have approached, you may go places you never would have gone, and you may try new things that would have terrified you before. It will surprise you. Just enjoy the ride!

As Fear falls away, your ability to trust yourself, others, and God increases by the same amount. Growing up, my identity was based on the False Self, and I walked around scared all the time. I made friends with everyone, yet did not have any level four or five friends because my relationships were based on Fear. I Feared that if I said or did the wrong thing, then those around me would stop being friends. I kept relations at the surface where it felt safe. I appeared happy all the time because I thought if I weren't smiling, people would not like me. The strategy worked for almost everyone...except for me. I performed well in school, but when I made mistakes, it crushed me because I thought I was disappointing someone. Looking back, I just shake my head and laugh. Of course, I acted that way, I learned it from my parents, and they learned it from theirs, and so on. The freedom I have experienced since those days has been unimaginable. I now see people for who they are instead of believing they will stop being friends with me for having a bad day, or thinking that strangers are out to get me. Remember, all people desire to feel loved, accepted, and safe. Their strategies may not be healthy, kind, or beneficial to relationships, but people are all just trying to get their needs met or protect themselves from being hurt further. Lastly, once you realize that God created you, knows your needs because He made you that way, and can meet your needs perfectly, then your ability to trust Him surges as well. These are all good things!

Take a moment to sit with what is coming up for you regarding Fear and Trust. What will you decide to do with the energy that is surfacing?

Gratitude versus Entitlement

I find it funny that entitlement (which is thinking we deserve something without having to earn it) is quickly pointed out in other people, but individuals have a hard time seeing it in themselves. Those of you from the older generations have probably taken note of a shift as the pendulum has swung toward more entitlement and less gratitude in the younger generations. It may be that every older generation sees this in younger generations, I am not sure. Regardless of the reason, the more you feel entitled about life, the more miserable you will be because life will constantly fail you. I hope you caught that: life will fail you and your expectations if you believe you deserve things you haven't earned.

What does entitlement look like in life? Believing that everything in your day should happen just like you planned. Thinking that everyone around you should do things perfectly, yet your mistakes should be given grace. Believing that you deserve an inheritance just for being a child of a wealthy parent. Believing that you deserve an additional reward beyond what you agreed upon for compensation. Thinking that you should have something just because everyone else does. Believing that everyone else should pay attention to you. Get the picture? The result of entitlement includes potentially debilitating negative emotions when you do not get your way, which leads to failed relationships and, ultimately, a lonely, miserable life.

On the other hand, you may be an individual who does not feel entitled. Actually, you feel as though you do not deserve anything. Perhaps, you tend to take pride in how much difficulty and heartache you can put yourself through to show just how *un*entitled you can be. You probably have a hard time receiving gifts because you did not earn them. Even though entitlement is not in your vocabulary, this is not a mindset of gratitude either. Gratitude brings freedom, not slavery.

A mindset of gratitude views life as a gift. A gift is not something you have to earn. A gift is not something you deserve, you can expect, or you can demand. A gift is something to be received and accepted with graciousness and with an appreciation for the giver's sacrifice and motivation despite how unworthy you feel to receive the gift. The gift is not about you, it is about the giver and their expression of wanting to share a piece of themselves with you.

Perhaps you do not feel unworthy, yet you still struggle with receiving gifts. You may fear the need to reciprocate with a gift of equal value. This could influence your mindset to not want to receive gifts because you feel in debt to the giver, thereby feeling controlled or manipulated. If the giver has strings attached to a gift, then it is not a gift at all, but a bribe. Use self-awareness when receiving a gift and recognize if your fear is based in truth and the gift actually is a bribe, or if your fear is unfounded (which often times you will find to be the case). A gift has no strings attached and can be received without fear of repayment. You are not in debt to the giver. They do not control you.

Genuine gratitude cannot be faked. An attitude of gratitude stems from a deep appreciation for all things gifted to you. Life. Each day. Every breath. Your body. Your abilities. Your relationships. If you view your life as a gift, then even the material possessions you have acquired can be labeled as gifts, regardless of how hard you worked to earn them. The abilities to learn and contribute to society through your work are gifts. Therefore, you could not have obtained your material possessions without such marvelous gifts. Even the wealthiest person in the world could never repay God for the gift of life. Thank goodness for our gift!

You get it, I know. So how do you develop an attitude of gratitude? Let us look at a few ways. Personally, I have made it a practice on my drive to work to, first, look up past the road to all that is around me (creating more self-awareness) and, second, thank God for all the many gifts and blessings in my life. Each prayer I make begins with gratitude. Others read their list of blessings each morning and each night to remind themselves of all their gifts. Replacing *have to* with *get to* is another tactic that has really helped many people, including me. For example, I don't *have to* go to work, I *get to* go to work; I don't *have to* eat a healthy meal, I *get to* eat a healthy meal. Above all, gratitude starts like all other changes in life. They start with intentionality (especially at first), to thank God even when you are not really feeling grateful. When you are running late for work, practice thanking God for a vehicle to get you to the job you are thankful for, as opposed to being hyper-focused on the slowpoke in front of you. When your kids are arguing, creating noise, and making messes, take a breath, thank God for your children, and *then* approach the kids. Ancient wisdom states that your words are the outpouring of your heart. Fill your heart with gratitude, and you will find that you appreciate yourself and others so much more.

My cousin has said for years, "My attitude is

contagious! And mine's worth catching!" This is also true. In our discussion of mirror neurons, we indicated that our body picks up on the smiles and attitudes of others. If you want to be surrounded by gratitude, you can help yourself by starting the trend and embodying an attitude of gratitude first. Watch the contagion spread!

Where on the spectrum of gratitude and entitlement do you currently find yourself? Which emotions are surfacing? Where do you feel them in your body? How does your place on the gratitude spectrum affect your relationships? Do you notice any urge to make a change toward gratitude? Witness your self-awareness without judgment. Do you want to plan for success with a more grateful heart? Take a moment now to do so, or make a note to come back to it later.

Other versus Self

I intentionally left this mindset for last. Many people struggle with recognizing and admitting to having a self-focused mindset. However, if you and I are honest with ourselves, we are more self-focused than other-focused. This is normal. It is our human nature. Why even have this as a mindset if everyone is self-focused? The goal of this mindset is balance, somewhere toward the middle, slightly on the side of self. Maybe it comes as a shock that I am suggesting you even be on the side of self at all. What happens when you reside on the other-focused side of the mindset? You will likely burn out over time because your body cannot keep up with the stress and demands that you and others continue to place on your shoulders. Or you carry on, yet experience problems with your body resulting in a stress-related autoimmune disease. Ideally, you will create an awareness of self that allows for self-care, while creating an awareness of others that cultivates empathy. We have discussed over and over the necessity of the balance of both self-care and empathy, which leads to feeling both healthy and happy living. What changes toward a more balanced self-focus and other-focus do you want to make?

Distorted Thinking

In addition to the nine mindsets detailed in this chapter, throughout the rest of the book I have addressed many of David Burns' common cognitive distortions found in cognitive behavioral therapy including all-or-nothing thinking, overgeneralizing, disqualifying the positive, emotional reasoning, minimization and magnification, labeling, and personalization. To complete a cognitive shift, I want to shine a spotlight on the final cognitive distortion called jumping to conclusions.

Jumping to Conclusions

Jumping to conclusions has had a history of wreaking havoc in people's lives and relationships for thousands of years. Jumping to conclusions combines emotional reasoning, or believing the lie *I feel, therefore, it is*, along with the ability to either read other people's minds or tell the future. The prognosis is usually despair. The first (and most common) problem with jumping to conclusions is mind reading, which is based on the misconception that you can know with 100% certainty what someone else thinks. For example, when you believe that someone at work does not like you because they looked away when you looked at them or some other nonverbal act. As a result, you feel rejected, hurt, and angry, which may be followed by the silent treatment or an argument. If this sounds familiar, I promise I do not have a camera installed in your home. Mind reading is common and can be devastating to relationships.

Imagine if you could actually read other people's minds. What would that be like? Would you want that ability? One thing you would notice if you could read minds is how much other people think almost exclusively about themselves and so little about you. A potential litmus test for knowing when you identify with your True Self is realizing that you have no desire to know what people think of you because what they think does not matter anymore. You have no control over what they believe. You only have power over being the best version of yourself to be who *you* want to be. This is just another freedom accompanying seeing your True Self.

The second aspect of jumping to conclusions is fortune telling or believing that you know something terrible is going to happen in the future. This allows Fear to take root, suppressing your possibilities for growth and a better future. Jumping to conclusions stifles relationships and leads to feeling miserable.

Do you want the ability to know the future and seeing everything that will happen in your future? How would that change your actions in the present? How would that, in turn, alter the future? This is a conundrum. Personally, I think life would be boring if I knew the future. No spice! Perhaps you do not agree. Specific little nuggets of information may be helpful to know, but if seeing the future was an all-or-nothing deal, I definitely choose nothing. Regardless, the fact remains that no human can read minds or tell the future. Everyone benefits when we stop trying, but in your case, you benefit most of all.

How do you stop? Create more self-awareness of the interior. When you recognize that you are assuming you know what someone else is thinking without them saying it, then speak truth against the misconception in the moment. Think back to when you were a child, and you were playing king of the mountain. Who usually won? The person with the best footing does. The truth and the Truth give you a solid foundation to stand on.

Sometimes I do not like the truth, I'll be honest. Do I like that my child's behavior is a stronger reflection of my relationship with them than their desire to act out? No, but it does not make it any less true. Do I like that I treat my family differently when I am stressed out, and I know it is my own lack of self-care that is causing the issue, and not their behavior? Definitely not. Even when you do not like the truth because it hurts or causes you to swallow your pride, the truth is no less relevant. However, if you continue to believe and feed into the lie, it can only support you for so long before it crumbles. You fall, you get hurt, those around you get hurt, and the crown goes to someone else with better footing.

What are you standing on?

Hello, Patience.

Cognitive restructuring of mindsets, distortions, limiting beliefs, and fears by seeking Truth.
Self-care through deep breathing, mindfulness, connection, guided imagery, art, drama, music, dance, and dreaming.
Self-awareness of your interior, exterior, and choice.
Healing brain and body through sleep, diet, movement, breathing, laughter, time in nature, and connectedness.
Communicating empathy, assertiveness, and collaboration.
Connectedness through interdependence.
Fear versus Faith/Trust. Purpose.
Identity. True Self. Love, Acceptance, and Trust/Safety.
Hope. Control. Self-responsibility. Priorities.

11

Lucky Living

This is the chapter you have been waiting for, the culmination of all that has been discussed about the iceberg under the water. Now we will focus on the visible tip of the iceberg sticking out of the water or behavioral change. This is your chance to be the person others call Lucky!

Building a Solid Structure

Each chapter has been building upon the previous as if we have been constructing a home. You need a foundation for a house to be strong and stable. This you found in chapters one and two, when you learned about establishing hope through understanding personal control, taking responsibility, and choosing to kick blame to the curb. In chapter three, you framed the house by believing in your True Self and understanding the inherent value we each possess. Then you put on a roof and siding as protection for the home as you learned to decrease your fear, increase your faith, and seek out significance. Connectedness acts like the drywall, and communication as the drywall tape and compound allowing for a smooth, consistent look throughout the house (that will eventually offer much comfort and trust to your family and all of your guests). Chapter seven discussed the body and its influence on change, which could be viewed as the flooring installed throughout the house, supporting each daily step in your home. Your new sense of awareness of the interior, exterior, and choice can be seen in all of the wall coverings, often forgotten, yet serving as a colorful reminder of the beauty missed each day without awareness. Self-care could be viewed as all the interior fixtures and furniture, creating your chosen environment for your home while setting the tone for each daily experience. As you bring your family into your house, the relationships, conversations, activities, and interactions determine the mood, just as our mindsets influence the emotions in your body. Finally, your behaviors (this chapter) can be likened to the exterior landscaping and yard, or the snapshot picture of the outside of the house that is visible to anyone looking.

As you drive down the road viewing house after house, you may think you know exactly what is going on inside the home just by judging the exterior compared to the acceptable social norms of your area, but that is not always a clear indicator. Sometimes the outside offers a reasonably accurate portrayal.

What do your behaviors indicate with regards to the inner workings of who you are and how you have or have not taken care of the inside of your house? Is there any congruency between the two? Spend some time with these two questions. They create the self-awareness crucial for being Lucky.

When most people think of change, they expect to be

able to see it manifested in a person's behaviors. Is that always true? Probably at least to some small degree. For example, when a person feels hopeless, their behaviors often mimic symptoms of depression. If that depressed person experienced hope for a better future, then their behavioral change may be revealed in the smile on their face, increased socialization, engagement in activities they enjoy, or eating and sleeping within normal limits. But, as you have read and now understand, humans are much more complicated than that.

Changing one aspect of your interior can manifest in significant change on the outside, but this is not to be expected. This necessitates *The Gift of Life* **experience**. Sometimes you feel substantial changes on the inside, but they are seen as subtle nuances to everyone around you (unless they really know you well). I expect that you have been feeling these changes within as hope, love, acceptance, value, trust, faith, self-awareness, and mindset shifts have taken root in your mind, body, and soul. From the outside, few may see how these alterations have rerouted the wiring of your brain and healed your heart. However, as control, responsibility, interdependence, empathy, assertiveness, collaboration, and self-care are assimilated into your being, then others will be acutely aware of your behavioral changes. Even if you started this journey motivated by accolades or recognition you may receive from outside yourself, by now you understand that being who you say you want to be is in many respects being Lucky. Therefore, this chapter is to help you reach personal goals. However, as a result, people will call you Lucky.

Measuring Change

Behavioral change, or any change seen from the outside by others through your actions, usually is measured by *consistency* and *longevity*. You can chart a new path in life, for example, start a new exercise routine, diet, bible reading routine (or the like) with a little bit of prep work and some gumption, but it may be that no one really believes you will follow through consistently for the long haul. Half the time *you* doubt your change will last, which we know plays into your success or lack thereof. Why do you seem to fall short of the behavioral changes you attempt in your life? Why do changes tend to be seen as short spurts of consistency? Let us look at short-term change.

Short-Term Change

Short-term change, or first-order change, can be accomplished by various means, but the roots are typically fertilized with fear, control, rewards, and consequences. As a child, how did your parents get you to do something?

Do it, or I will spank your butt!

Do it because I said so!

I will give you a prize if you do it!

If you don't do it, then you lose your favorite thing for a week!

Do any of these statements sound familiar? Not only did my parents use these, but I also found myself saying the same things all the time when my older children were much younger. I thought these techniques were "good parenting." I believed my teaching would instill respect and discipline while building a strong character. However, I had not been presented with the whole picture yet. Can you see the fear, control, rewards, and consequences? Reread these statements and witness what is coming up for you. Sit with your own memories and emotions for a moment.

Some memories of your childhood may surface. The memories may be accompanied by some subtle or intense emotions. Which emotions are filling your chest, your gut, or your head at this moment? Often people experience fear, anger, resentment, shame, or other negative emotions. After reading the previous exclamatory parental statements, do you feel more motivated? Most do not. Perhaps you do. If so, can you sense that the motivation has been joined by the emotion of guilt?

Don't get me wrong; in both leadership and in parenting, rewards and consequences play an essential role in follow-through. However, to create second-order change, you need more than these basic behavioral techniques. Fear and control will work for a time for many kids and even some adults (accompanied by great distress). Other options exist that empower people and lead to more consistency and longevity. Over the long-term, we know that fear decreases faith and trust in a parent or leader while it creates anxiety and depression in the person due to the focus on the False Self. These are not the messages you want to embody yourself, teach your child, or communicate to other adults if you desire full potential to blossom.

What other options are beyond using fear, control, rewards, and consequences or (as they are experienced) fear, guilt, shame, anxiety, and depression? The rest of the chapter will lay out a practical approach incorporating everything you have learned on our journey together.

Long-term Change

What does it take to generate long-term, second-order change in yourself? To begin, you need your success plan, of course! Without a clearly defined goal and concurrent strategy, you will be directionless, scattered, following feelings and intuition instead of utilizing your full potential. We discussed *who* you are (values), *where* you want to go (your vision), and *what* are the reasons (your mission) in chapter one. All the chapters since have solidified those. Now we can discuss *how* you will get there.

Often individuals use the acronym SMART to describe *how*. SMART stands for Specific, Measurable, Achievable, Relevant, and Time-bound, to clearly define their strategy.

Specific answers the question: what is my goal?

Measurable answers the question: how do I know when I have reached my goal?

Achievable answers the question: does it seem possible with the tools and resources available?

Relevant answers the question: does this goal actually get me to where I want to be?

Time-bound answers the question: when will I do it?

Do you have to use SMART goals? As long as you are addressing all the fundamental aspects of goal planning, use any framework that works for you. However, SMART covers some of the rudimentary characteristics of a strategy. Let us begin by breaking down the SMART acronym into bite-size pieces to understand everything going on here.

Specific

Your *Specific* goal incorporates giving yourself permission to dream. This is the fun part! Savor the energy of dreaming with a partner, getting excited about future possibilities, and envisioning what life could be like after the change. Some of my fondest memories are sitting around campfires dreaming with my wife and friends.

When did you last allow yourself to dream big? What was the dream? As you witness what is coming up within you right now, you may experience the same excited energy I feel each time I create space to dream big. Bottle the energy by closing your eyes, visualizing the future in as much detail as possible, and then write it down in your idea notebook. If you do not have an idea notebook, then consider acquiring one. Whenever you need a boost of energy through excitement to get you to the next step, then bring out the notebook and experience it all over again by remembering what first drew you in and wooed you into falling in love with the idea. Keep the notebook close by, because you may need the encouragement often. I use mine daily. Use the dream and vision you create to shape your *Specific* goal.

As you dream about an unknown future, you may recognize a familiar voice inside speaking all kinds of negativity. If this is the case, then begin organizing your house. Start with hope. Are doubts of accomplishing meaningful change in your life originating from a lack of hope? What do you do with a lack of hope? Start by assessing what you have control over and what you have no control over. Remember, you have no power over others or the outcome of the future. You have control over your choices and planning for success. When you focus on what you have no control over, this is when your hope will diminish due to allowing Fear to take root, leading to anxiety. Identify the Fear holding you hostage, or the voice that is screaming that you could never have the money, the resources, the help, the competency, the ability, or any of many other disempowering doubts. Then take a moment and write down the truth about the fear, to defeat any lies surfacing.

Are there legitimate risks to take part in substantial change? Absolute! Without question. However, nothing incredible in life happens without risk, sacrifice, or investment. Think of anything extremely amazing in your life, and I can guarantee it took risk, sacrifice, investment, and a load of hard work. Do you want to wait for Luck to happen to you, or do you want to create Luck? The whole point of this book is to offer you the gift of creating your own Luck, as opposed to allowing life to pass by as you hang your hope on something entirely out of your control (that may never even happen). You can create your own Luck! Let's get to it and embrace being Lucky!

In my journey of writing this book, the fears of failure that I had to fight included: *You will not complete the book. This model will not actually help anyone. No one will join you in your vision. You will not succeed!* Of course, these cognitive distortions fall under the label of fortune telling. I spoke truth to them. *I have no control over the future, except for my plan.* Therefore, I focused on the plan. Each and every night my alarm was set to wake up early to write. When an appointment failed to show at work, and paperwork did not flood my desk, I wrote. I continued to dream with my dream partners and focused on growing the idea to the best of my abilities. Hundreds of hours were sacrificed. Definitely risky business when you are not guaranteed a return on your investment, but I personally grew through the entire process, which made the sacrifice worth every moment.

All plans include risk, but taking responsibility for what you have control over through planning will allow you to mitigate a certain amount of risk and increase the chance of a successful leap of faith.

Measurable

As you are planning your goal and creating a measurable way to know when you have reached your goal, you painstakingly evaluate the financial calculations, time calculations, and future maneuvers. With any vision, assess the balance between your measurable goal's bullseye and what it is worth to you as an investment of time, talent, and treasure. Few plans work out as written, but without a plan, you are on a treasure hunt without a map, wandering aimlessly toward an unknown location, hoping for a payoff that will likely lead to disappointment. You are not that pirate!

As you stoke the fire of hope and excitement, the next step is to break your vision down into *Measurable* benchmarks. This will include proactive consideration of your needs. How much time, energy, resources, etc. will you need to create a successful vision? If your plan is not bringing about your vision successfully, then rework your plan. Brainstorm every possibility (even ideas that don't make sense). Begin again and repeat. Remember, people don't fail, plans fail. People just give up on their plans and allow their visions and dreams to die. Commit now to be part of the few that don't give up, and you will be Lucky!

In creating your plan, many questions need to be answered:

What is a reasonable timeline to help me create my vision?

What is a reasonable financial plan?

What resources do I need?

How does this measurable plan fit in to who I want to be?

What is my time worth?

How am I able to continue my current responsibilities while creating this vision?

What responsibilities need to be de-prioritized during this season?

These questions may seem daunting at first, but know that you are not alone. You can find individuals interested in your vision to help answer these questions, in addition to any that will inherently follow. Consider taking this to heart: you don't have to be a lone ranger, but you will have to be a leader. You can only be a leader if you are connected with others. Find your group.

Achievable

Achievable acknowledges that you have done your planning homework and can see that on paper your goal looks attainable through your strategy. In addition to the physical plan, you are also looking in your house at the characteristics of value and identity. You may hold a polished, strategic design in your hands ready to leap, but if you look in the mirror and only see the False Self reflecting back, then, plainly said: you are not prepared. Consider spending extra time in chapter two, as well as spending time connected to others who believe in possibility through hard work. Recognizing your inherent value and rooting your identity in your True Self (as opposed to basing it off of the failures of who you have been) create the foundation for an *Achievable* goal.

What if you have a fantastic plan and a firm foundation, but you lack competence, ability, or credibility? Education or training may be needed. The last thing you may want to do is invest loads of time, energy, and resources, however investing in your future self through education and training will lead to reaping the benefits during the process, the rest of your life, and potentially for generations to come! Further, the journey of growth experienced through your educational investment will give you something to look forward to, dream about, and will keep the excitement afire. Lucky people are driven by being who they say they want to be and are life-long learners (growth mindset). Take hold of your chance to be who you say you want to be and make your goal *Achievable* through education and training, if necessary.

Lastly, assume that your strategic plan will change throughout the journey. This is not a failure! If your plan lacks change, then you are not allowing your goal to be the best version of itself. What may seem *Achievable* today may be different tomorrow. It may seem as though your plan changes weekly if not daily. For example, most of the time, writing this book was priority number one during my scheduled time to write. However, to make the book and business model successful, at times I was called away from writing to work on the website, revamp the workshop, reach out to others for help, research, or one of many other personal or familial needs. Planning to learn from things that are not working, rewriting the plan as often as needed, and seeing your True Self through the process will give your plan the best chance of being *Achievable,* not just at the beginning but all the way until you reach the finish line.

Relevant

Next, *Relevant* integrates finding purpose and meaning in your vision and goals, which coincides with the next step in managing your internal house. Your motivation to accomplish a goal becomes magnified with the level of purpose you see within the objective. Think about the reason people put themselves in uncomfortable situations, like going door to door to talk to people about Jesus. They are driven by the purpose of saving people from an eternity absent of the presence of God. Can you see how *Relevant* their purpose is to them? What have you done in your life that was unhindered by Fear as a result of finding the experience purposeful?

Regardless of what it is, keep your true purpose close to your heart, to recognize the *Relevance* of your goal, and motivation will join purpose in your heart space. This will not be the case if you focus on financial gain. Research has shown time and again how money lacks the power to motivate most people to work at their best every day. Money is not purpose, money is just another tool. You make money, and you spend money. You make more money, and you spend more money. Finding purpose in what you do, however, is priceless.

Lastly, *Time-bound* seems relatively self-explanatory and brings us back to the timeline strategy in your *Measurable* plan. I didn't say SMART was a perfect acronym. Besides SMAR just looks weird.

The Gift of Luck SMART goal

If you condense my personal goal into an easy to read format, the first draft of my SMART goal of writing this book looked similar to the following:

Specific: My goal is to write a book that will act as the tool by which I can create a worldwide movement of change through coaching individuals with *The Gift of Luck* model and certifying individuals as Satellites of Change through the ICHWC.

Measureable: I will know that I have met this goal when *The Gift of Luck* book is published, when I am offering one or two workshops per month, and when I am coaching and training.

Achievable: I have the competency, ability, motivation, support, tools, resources, and credibility to be able to achieve my goals due to my formal education, certifications and licenses, personal and professional experiences, and community of support.

Relevant: I find meaning in offering others *The Gift of Luck* message, which will help individuals, families, communities, countries, and the world change for good. I am creating *The Gift of Luck* to be a part of something bigger than myself while connecting with people and the divine.

Time-bound: My business model will be completed within a year of publishing *The Gift of Luck* book.

A SMART goal contains multiple factors of behavior

change, just like an iceberg under the water. Hope. Control. Personal responsibility. Value. Identity. Purpose. Fear. Faith. Trust. Good reasons to start with a SMART goal? I think so. By now these words look familiar, and you may already know the next factor of behavioral change, right? Yep. The need for connection to assist in behavioral change.

Change Connection

Have you ever had anyone in your life consistently cheerlead you on toward your goals? What has been your experience of being on the receiving end of such a gift? Imagine that your parents created a container for you where you always knew that they were For you and With you, regardless of the outcome of reaching a goal. Instead of disapproval, you would be met with encouragement. You would not be faced with disappointment, but love and acceptance. You would know that they would tell you the hard truth assertively, with love, and not as a way to guilt or shame. No matter what mistakes you made in your life, you would know your parents would consistently be by your side. What would that mean to you? How much more likely would you have been to listen to what they had to say when they offered pearls of wisdom, nuggets of knowledge, and suggestions about how to learn from their past or their perspective of your life? How does respect play out in this scenario? When parents are For their kids and With their kids, the kids will seek out guidance from their parents due to the high level of respect, love, acceptance, safety, and consistency.

Adults are just big kids! We were created to need a caregiver who is For us and With us, regardless of our mistakes, helping us learn, grow, and encouraging us toward greatness. You can feel that inside, can't you? The warmth in your chest that spreads out from the center like a sun radiating as it increases your heart rate and almost takes your breath away. Tap into the emotion, create more awareness of your interior, and allow it to draw you close. I promise you won't stay there forever. You may need a moment with Patience before moving on.

Hello, Patience.

How does this translate into accomplishing your current life goals, overcoming challenges, and making changes? Simply stated: you need people. You need people who are For you and With you. Some people would call this an accountability partner. This could fit the bill. Often people pick accountability partners working toward the same goal, but it is essential to choose an accountability partner uninvolved with your goal or find a second accountability partner.

Think back to your school days when you participated in a sport, drama team, musical group, church group, or some other activity with a goal in mind. You had a coach. Hopefully, someone you trusted, offering an outside perspective, who you knew wanted what was best for you and the team. The teammates struggling beside you could be encouraging while building a social community (which are both highly treasured), but they could not see the bigger picture (just as you could not). Think of it as trying to read the label on a jar when you are in the jar. It simply does not work. Your coach could read the label and see the big picture, assertively tell you the truth, ask questions that propelled you forward, and make suggestions that could potentially raise you to the next level. Even if you have never experienced a proper coach in your life, such a person could be invaluable for personal growth and change. Do you have anyone in your life who could play such a role?

Our family, friends, and spouses can be great for such a role if they can offer these crucial ingredients: unconditional support (love), a non-judgmental attitude and a focus on the True Self (acceptance), the capability to help maneuver through or around obstacles (safety), showing up when they say they will show up (consistency and commitment), the ability to speak truth in love (assertiveness), and the capacity to ask powerful questions. However, be honest with yourself and them regarding the feasibility of the relationship. Their role could draw you closer to them than you have ever experienced. However, the opposite threat exists if either of you is not ready. Sometimes, hiring a life coach (or the like) can be easier. You decide what your goal is worth regarding time, money, return on invest, etc. and make a Lucky choice.

If you do have someone in your world who can or has acted as your coach, then consider yourself blessed. Foster a reciprocal relationship with this person, where they feel neither used nor neglected, and do your best to create the container for them. Such connections are unique and infinitely precious. Please treat them as such. It is appropriate to stop reading and reach out in gratitude to your person right now before any other thoughts or distractions steal the limelight of your attention. Committing to such a practice of immediate, intentional positivity in relationships transforms your heart, which creates a ripple effect in many other areas of your life.

I know the message of how people and relationships

are vital to life and success has been clear, consistent, and maybe even a bit annoying throughout this book. Actually, many messages have been hammered over and over. This is intentional. If you are an average person, you have to hear a message multiple times before it really takes root, you can effectively apply it to your life, and the fruits of the application are apparent in your behaviors. You add another layer of pavement to your neural pathways each time you read the message, process the message, and conceptualize the application to your life.

We need people. Got it!

Who is on your Lucky team?

Change Awareness

The next aspect of long-term change requires using your awareness of interior, exterior, and choice. You will notice that you will change through the journey of pursuing your goal (as will your SMART plan). Self-awareness enhances both you and your outcome, which develops through powerful questions.

Awareness of Interior

The hardest part of answering probing questions is being honest with yourself, and not explaining what you want to believe to be true. Think about the following self-awareness of the interior questions to help mold your SMART goals:

Who am I completing my goal for?

What is really motivating me to reach my goal?

If I have attempted this goal in the past, what thoughts, beliefs, fears, emotions, or personal behaviors have pushed against me as I tried to move toward my goal?

What am I willing to sacrifice in order to reach my goal?

What priority roles (at home, work, or elsewhere) am I neglecting and need to reprioritize?

How can I live a more balanced life?

What is my body telling me I need?

What past choices can I learn from to reach my goal?

Which relationships are helping or limiting in the pursuit of my goal?

How do I need to change to be more intentional about reciprocity in my relationships?

How empathetic have I been for myself and others while striving toward my goal?

When (and with who) can I spend more time dreaming?

How is my goal bringing me closer to experiencing the positive emotions I desire?

What stones do I still need to toss?

In chapter eight we discussed the importance of being aware of your body and emotions throughout the process of life. This truth becomes exponentially more vital when working toward a goal. Spending those moments with Patience, listening to your body, discerning its language, and embracing what it communicates sets a healthy pace in a way that works for you. No one else will have the exact flow that you need. That is okay. Give yourself the gift of experiencing all your emotions as you forge through the process of completing each task. Wisdom can be found at the heart of your emotions.

While in the midst of your journey, remember to become aware of your True Self, spirit, and attunement with

God in respect to your goal. Often the question of God's will comes into play at this point. Scheduling time consistently to be still and silent while meditating and praying creates a relational conversation within and with God, which leads to the awareness and clarity necessary to be able to answer the question of God's will for a specific timeframe. Seek, ask, listen, and be honest about the conversation. If you need more clarity, seek out others you trust, who you feel are attuned with God. I cannot tell you how many times God has used others to speak truth, knowledge, wisdom, and confirmation to me. Keep your eyes peeled, ears open, growth mindset turned on, meditation and prayer consistent, self-awareness attuned, and the message will be clear. Your willingness to hear the message remains to be the most challenging part for most (myself included).

Awareness of Exterior

One moment standing in my kitchen with my wife has imprinted itself in my mind. She stated, "You are just not here." I didn't quite understand as I asked, "What am I doing wrong?" She replied in a clear, yet nonjudgmental tone, "You are going through the motions just fine. You do your part. But *you* are just not here." She was right. My thoughts were consumed with work, and even though I still took responsibility for my roles at home, my mind had disengaged from the actions of my body. After an initial defensive response, I pledged to myself (and later to my wife) to be more mindful of the moments with her and with our kids.

How often do you need someone you trust to give you a wakeup call to awareness? Do you allow anyone to help you recognize ways you are limiting yourself or even hurting yourself? Such vulnerability requires a high level of trust. Consider giving those in your level five the permission to speak truth even when the truth may be painful. This only stings for a moment, but the benefits could better your entire life for good. Although the responsibility lies on your shoulders to become aware of yourself, being open to learning from others will secure a more prosperous future. This is a great way to enhance awareness of the interior and exterior.

Another aspect of becoming aware of your exterior is through the lens of your barriers. What barriers keep you from your goal? Barriers are anything outside of yourself that have, in the past, rerouted your success plan away from the target. Barriers are often visual, auditory, relational, situational, or even time related. When you hear a particular song, and the tune reminds you of a past version of yourself or previous personal failure. Being around people who smoke when you are trying to quit. Seeing pictures from your past. Often, being alone and left to your own ruminations can be the greatest barrier of all, although it doesn't have to be.

You have two choices when it comes to barriers. Avoid them or overcome them. Some barriers linked to addiction are likely too substantial for a former addict to conquer at first. Their best plan could be to figuratively and literally run the other way! Some barriers are unavoidable. For example, even though you may be told by your doctor to avoid sugar, I doubt television advertisers received the message to stop airing commercials that promote sugary products. Unavoidable barriers will need to be overcome with the help of your person, your people, your strategic plan, and being Lucky. With time and support, each barrier can be broken down, even if brick by brick. They only have power if we give them power. However, you have to be honest with yourself, *genuinely* honest with yourself, and others to get to a place of such life-changing freedom. As previously mentioned, people do not fail, only plans fail, and when people fail to plan, they choose failure. How true has this been in your life? You are made for so much more!

The most significant barrier that kept me from pursuing my goals with *The Gift of Luck* included binge-watching Netflix. After a long day, I enjoyed watching a show or movie to allow my brain to disconnect before going to bed. The problem arose when I would get sucked into the vortex that the commercial-free, instant gratification of Netflix offers. One show became three or many more. As a result, I was forced to decide between sleep and pursuing my goals, because the time I typically slept had somehow disappeared.

The other unfortunate reality of situations similar to this is that the effects quickly compound. When one poor choice turns into two, and potentially many more. Before you know it, steps have not been taken toward your goal in a week or two, which influences you to give up. Through awareness, I have been forced to make a choice to get less sleep (which makes for a harder day) to stay on track from my binge or skip the binge. Does this scenario sound familiar?

What if you find little to no support in those around you, which further influences you to feel like they are holding you back from your goal and pursuit of purpose? This is a tough question to answer. However, as a rule of thumb, if you seek a goal, then surround yourself with others who pursue goals and purpose, which will likely add momentum toward being Lucky. If those around you who pursue goals and purpose still discourage your vision, then try to discern if they are acting out of fear or love. Those operating out of fear will present reasons filled with emotional rationality and possibly personal bias. However, if their justification is based on facts and they respond with tough questions to answer, then take pause. This is not to say that you cannot step out in faith, but do your best to step out in faith while doing your preparatory part.

Awareness of Choice

Self-awareness of choice flows out of your awareness of interior and exterior and can be embraced as an enemy or as an ally. As an enemy, your choices have the power to ruin your life and/or those around you and, unfortunately, one decision can accomplish such a feat. For example, if you are married with kids in a home with a good job then, first of all, you are blessed and, secondly, you understand that one poor choice of infidelity can ruin everything. Choices are powerful! As an ally, one decision can propel you into a life-changing future for good, as well. How do you currently utilize awareness of choice for your goals (enemy or ally)?

Preparation empowers you with control, and the chance to get comfortable to make those life-giving choices. Two questions need to be answered to create an awareness of choice while attempting to manifest an investment mindset:

Who do I want to be?

Is this choice getting me closer to who I want to be?

Plan to ask these questions daily, hourly, or even moment to moment, when needed. Being Lucky is directly linked to your self-awareness of the interior, exterior, and choice.

Hello, Patience.

Change Beliefs

How do mindsets come into play when achieving a behavioral change goal and being Lucky? As you are becoming keenly aware, all of the underlying factors previously discussed in attaining a goal are both created and affected by our thoughts, beliefs, and mindsets. View mindset as a spiraling up or spiraling down effect. For example, hope influences a spiraling up of healthy mindsets and beliefs, which in turn fuels more hope and more healthy mindsets and more hope, and so on. Our healthy mindsets produce healthy behaviors, and goals become attainable. Conversely, when you start feeling hopeless, it can influence a spiraling down into unhealthy thoughts, beliefs, and mindsets. The result is not Lucky.

The truths you believe will make or break your goal attainment, and your mindsets will either fuel progress or extinguish your flame of motivation. To be Lucky, many important truths to need to be accepted into your belief system:

You can accomplish your goal when you focus on what you have control over.

Your past mistakes give you more of an edge because you learned what did not work.

You are valuable regardless of your behavioral change because your True Self is not your behaviors.

Fear is a façade that you create; fear is not real, and it will hold you back from your behavior change unless you fight fear with truth, faith, and trust.

You need people to support you in completing your behavioral change.

God is For you, With you, wants what is best for you, and He works out His good plan through those who love him and follow Him.

You can be the one to stop generational problems and begin generational blessing.

Emotions are always good and help us to build empathy for others.

You need to care for yourself to be able to care for others well.

You may find specific truths that speak to you, but remember to express the truth about hope and control, value and identity, fear and faith, purpose, connectedness, family of origin, awareness, empathy, and self-care. Review the fundamental mindsets and notice which ones may hold you back from attaining your specific behavior change goal.

Behavior change almost always begins with a catalyst. Your catalyst may include someone making fun of you, someone demanding you to change "or else," your dislike for aspects of personal thoughts, emotions, behaviors, and relationships, or one of a multitude of other negative reasons. Even if a negative catalyst started your journey, positive psychology suggests that positive catalysts tend to result in longer lasting change than negative catalysts. Therefore, take your negative catalyst and reframe it into something positive, and something you have control over. Ultimately, recognize that your change is for you because you are working toward who you want to be. Changing for others can be incredibly motivating, especially when you really do not see your True Self and value, however, even if you attain your goal you have no control over the other person's reaction to your change. Your best plan includes working through all of the underlying roots of being Lucky to create a lifetime of growth, learning, and opportunity because you want to be *that* person. Try that perspective on for size.

This is who I want to be. These words have helped immensely throughout my journey. On those days I did not want to get up after a Netflix binge. Defeating Fear daily. Ensuring follow-through in relationships despite falling short of my success plan for the day or week. Beginning the day with silence and solitude regardless of the time it would take away from my plan. The list goes on and on. Allow these words to be a North Star to you in your success plan and in life. You will not regret it. Consider these words to act as a *helping mindset* versus a limiting mindset.

You gain education through your life experiences, and your future offers the same benefits with a growth mindset. To be Lucky, consistently assess what works and what does not. Learn from that. You will make mistakes, but as you allow the mistakes to turn into learning experiences, then you master the *growth mindset*. To grow, change, and thrive, plan to stay on top of that learning curve.

As a leader, I am sure you have encountered roadblocks. People do not follow through on what they say they will do, star players move on, fires, tornadoes, and floods occur, bad investments happen, etc. Looking for the opportunity in the roadblock allows you to think outside the box, which can lead toward greatness. Further, looking for the opportunities even when no barriers are in front of you (except your own fear) requires a reframing toward an *opportunity mindset*. Building relationships with those around you when it is not comfortable or sharing your story with someone you just met are both opportunity mindset behavior changes that can enhance your chances of success. What roadblocks are keeping you from your goals right now? How can you reframe them into opportunities?

When barriers stand in your way, you could quickly become frustrated and throw blame around. How does blame allow you to achieve your goal? I knew you were learning! You are right, it doesn't. *Responsibility mindset* will help you step toward your goal. Continuously focusing on other's shortcomings is a way to justify your thoughts, emotions, and behaviors, but it keeps you in the pit with no way out. What do you need to reframe that will allow you to stop acting like a victim and instead act out a responsibility mindset? This will get you closer to your behavior change and being Lucky.

Throughout this book, you have read the words, "Invest in your future self." Your behavior change will require you to take that step of embodying an *investment mindset* by investing time, resources, and energy. Does your investment end there? Absolutely not! You will be challenged to make decisions daily that requires you to think of the long game for your goal. Building a relationship with someone, as opposed to using them to get what you want, can be a great example of an investment mindset versus an instant mindset. In what ways are you in need of an investment mindset to reach your goal of behavioral change?

What single factor most enslaves you, holds you captive, and keeps you from creating a life of significance and leaving a legacy of blessings to the future generations of your family? Yes, Fear. I am so proud! Fear keeps you sitting in an unlocked jail cell, consenting to waste your life, leaving your potential unfulfilled, and disregarding your calling for the sake of a False Self. Any behavioral change goes unaccomplished without a *trust mindset* and *faith mindset*. Trust yourself that you have what it takes to meet the moment-to-moment challenges, trust others to support you through the trials, and have faith that as you pursue God, He will act out His good purpose through you. The basis of life rests in relationship: a healthy relationship with yourself, healthy relationships with those around you, and a healthy relationship with God. If you get relationship right, you win! Your prize is embodied love, joy, peace, Patience, kindness, goodness, faithfulness, gentleness, and self-control. What Fear is worth the opportunity cost of passing up on such gifts?

A gift, by definition, is something you receive yet you did not work for. Do you deserve anything you haven't earned? Do you deserve food without having to buy it? Do you deserve a roof over your head without having a job to pay for it? Do you deserve to have your loved ones live when people around you have had theirs stolen away by death? Do you deserve a healthy working mind when others have been born without one? Do you deserve to live free when others are slaves to the dictators in their countries? Do you really deserve anything? Your answer will indicate the level to which you have a *gratitude mindset*. Entitlement, or believing you deserve anything you did not earn, leads to misery because you will always be let down.

You did not earn life, it was a gift. Times or even seasons in your life may have resulted in wanting to give the gift of your breath away. Perhaps it has been your whole life to this point. Wherever you came from, or whatever your story, your past is only the starting point, not your destination. It is time to rewrite the rest of your story. With a gratitude mindset, every day feels like Christmas because you are given gifts all day long. Any behavioral change feels more manageable when every moment has a built-in reward. Is there any hint of entitlement holding you back from the blessings of gratefulness, reaching your behavior change, and being Lucky?

Are you grateful for the people in your life? Balancing out your *other versus self mindset* can be tricky when you are working toward a behavior change goal. Sometimes your focus may be narrowed to only what you want to accomplish, and you forget your integral part in other people's change stories. You live in an interdependent web of life. Other times you focus too much on helping others, which leads to short-changing your own self-care time, feeling unappreciated, and experiencing burning out. The balance is real. Your balance in this mindset will be the fuel or the hindrance to achieving your goal. What does the idealistic balance of other versus self look like in your world? How can you leverage it to your benefit, the benefit of others, and the benefit of your goal?

Hello, Patience.

Behavior Math

You have now reviewed all of the tools and tactics involved in behavioral change using *The Gift of Luck* model. There is one last truth about behavior change that you need to understand. It is the simple truth that your behaviors are the result of all of the underlying aspects of who you are, and how you manage everything in chapters one through ten of this book. If it were a math equation, you would line up all of the aspects of self discussed thus far in this book on the left side of the equal sign, and on the right side is your behavior. If you were constructing a machine, then think about all the time, energy, and resources you would spend in building the machine, and these can be seen as the building blocks of hope and control all the way through this book to mindsets. How well the machine works is your behavior. *Behavior is just the output from all of the other inputs.* If something does not perform as expected, then something in the underlying mechanics is at fault, not the behavior itself. Behavior is just a communication tool. It communicates how well everything else underneath is functioning.

What do your behaviors communicate to the world about your hope, control, self-responsibility, identity, value, purpose, priorities, faith, fear, trust, connectedness, relational strategies, physical and genetic characteristics, self-awareness, self-care, beliefs, and mindsets?

Behavior Change as a result of long-term change tactics.
Cognitive restructuring of mindsets, distortions, limiting beliefs, and fears by seeking Truth.
Self-care through deep breathing, mindfulness, connection, guided imagery, art, drama, music, dance, and dreaming.
Self-awareness of your interior, exterior, and choice.
Healing brain and body through sleep, diet, movement, breathing, laughter, time in nature, and connectedness.
Communicating empathy, assertiveness, and collaboration.
Connectedness through interdependence.
Fear versus Faith/Trust. Purpose.
Identity. True Self. Love, Acceptance, and Trust/Safety.
Hope. Control. Self-responsibility. Priorities.

12

Your Lucky Change Story

Our journey has concentrated on exploring *your* growth potential and how to offer *you* the tools to discover *your* path to wholeness. I hope that this journey has furthered you toward your own personal goals and that it will continue to be a guiding light for the rest of your life to remind you of your True Self full-potential.

In this final chapter, I desire to encourage you to create your Lucky change story worth telling. Of course, you can only tell a good story if you have something to share and you have people to say it to. It is time to live out your Lucky life! Indeed, no matter your age, gender, ethnicity, education level, or residing location, you have a circle of influence. If you are a son or daughter, sibling, cousin, parent, or friend, then someone looks to you as an influence in their life, regardless if you want them to or not. This must be accepted. You impact every person you come into contact with. If you have received a position of leadership, then you have even more potential impact. The question to ask yourself is: *How will I use my Lucky change story to influence for good?*

If you find only ten people to share your Lucky change

story and *The Gift of Luck*, then the results could be world-altering. This multiplicity allows us together to make a considerable impact toward a better world. Not just a human race that accomplishes more or becomes more profitable (even though I believe those could be natural side effects), but the process includes more about understanding people, mirroring for them the truth of who they are, and helping them fulfill their purpose by aligning it with other like-minded individuals. Watch the movement of change sweep through your circle of influence, community, state, country, and beyond. Imagine what it would be like to have individuals everywhere you go practicing empathy, assertiveness, collaboration, and interdependence as love and acceptance abound within each person and through each person. Can you see it? Could this be a reality? There is only one way to find out. What do you have control over?

Who are the ten people you want to influence? How will you reach them? When will you take the first step?

1. _____
2. _____
3. _____
4. _____
5. _____
6. _____
7. _____
8. _____
9. _____
10. _____

Now that your list is complete, you can create the opportunity to share your Lucky change story with them. Everyone wants to know how to make their life more Lucky!

Begin by sharing what life was like before you began the journey.

_____

_____

_____

_____

_____

_____

_____

_____

_____

_____

_____

_____

_____

_____

_____

_____

_____

_____

Identify what aspects of the adventure impacted you most and in what ways. We are constantly learning and growing. Therefore, you will continue to add to this list as time progresses.

- Patience: _____
- Hope: _____
- Control: _____
- Responsibility: _____
- Priorities: _____
- Self-Love: _____
- Self-Acceptance: _____
- Self-Trust: _____
- Other-Love: _____
- Other-Acceptance: _____
- Other-Trust: _____
- Faith: _____
- Purpose: _____
- Connectedness: _____
- Interdependence: _____
- Empathy: _____
- Assertiveness: _____
- Collaboration: _____
- Sleep: _____
- Diet: _____

- Movement: _____

- Laughter: _____

- Time in Nature: _____

- Interior Awareness: _____

- Exterior Awareness: _____

- Choice Awareness: _____

- Self-Care: _____

- Growth mindset: _____

- Opportunity mindset: _____

- Helping mindset: _____

- Investment mindset: _____

- Optimist mindset: _____

- Responsibility mindset: _____

- Trust mindset: _____

- Gratitude mindset: _____

- Other mindset: _____

- _____

- _____

- _____

- _____

- _____

- _____

- _____

Next, describe how life has been since changing these areas of your life.

_____

_____

_____

_____

_____

_____

_____

_____

_____

_____

_____

_____

_____

_____

_____

_____

_____

_____

_____

_____

Lastly, express the areas in which you want to continue to intentionally pursue change. No need to keep it to the previous list. Dream big! Let your heart pour out its desires.

_____

_____

_____

_____

_____

_____

_____

_____

_____

_____

_____

_____

_____

_____

_____

_____

_____

_____

_____

_____

_____

_____

As the curtain closes for this act in our story together, I want to remember our first moments together as I would enjoy the delicate aroma of opening a bag of freshly-roasted coffee. I asked you if our meeting could be coincidence. Did Luck bring us together? Perhaps. Did Luck lead you through your incredible adventure of growth these twelve chapters? No, *you* did. Any Luck you have experienced as a result of your journey was due to your creation of Luck. This is your new Lucky life!

You and I both now know that Luck only exists in those living the fullness of life's calling and freedom from Fear. Life is too short to wait for Luck beyond our control. Create Luck, live out your highest potential, and many will call you Lucky. Only you will understand that to judge them for their ignorance seals their state for a little longer. Take the knowledge, experience, and wisdom you gained here and use it for the benefit of those with whom you live and those you love to act as a model for a better family and community. Be the light in the darkness. Pass your flame along to ignite a blaze unseen to date. Change will be ours.

Live Lucky!

About the Author: Blake Suzelis

When I decided to return to college for my Master's in Professional Counseling, after spending years running businesses, I didn't realize I signed up for heart surgery and a brain transplant. Even though it was not comfortable and I had to face parts of me I didn't know that I didn't know, the knowledge and wisdom gained has altered my life, all the lives around me, and it will continue to influence my family for many generations to come. The power of personal change!

I am now living in Wenatchee, Washington with my wife and five children while completing a PhD in Mind-Body Medicine. I am a Washington State Licensed Mental Health Counselor (LMHC), Child Mental Health Specialist (CMHS), Ohio State Licensed Professional Counselor (LPC), and Certified Clinical Trauma Professional (CCTP). In Ohio, I worked as a therapist at a behavioral counseling center for adults. For the next two and a half years, I owned Integrative Mental Health Counseling, LLC and acted as the sole practitioner serving primarily adults for trauma, anxiety, depression, and relationship counseling. After moving to Washington, my experience was rounded out by serving children and their families as a child and family therapist. After 18 months, I was promoted to the Supervisor of the WISe program, an intensive program for the at-risk youth and families. When Wenatchee opened an adult in-patient facility, I joined the team as their night therapist assisting individuals with severe trauma, mental health issues, and detox.

As the sole proprietor of Blake Suzelis Holistic Counseling, LLC, I serve children and adults as part of a holistic approach to healing, in addition to offering coaching, retreats, and trainings. Visit blakesuzelis.com for more details.

65988335R00156

Made in the USA
Middletown, DE
05 September 2019